EACH ONE
Reach One

A
Study
of
Church Growth
and
Personal Evangelism

Second Edition
(Revised and Enlarged)

Andrew D. Erwin

COBB PUBLISHING
Charleston, AR:
2017

Gospel Gleaner Publications
PO Box 456
Fayetteville, TN 37334
www.gospelgleaner.com
andyerwin@gospelgleaner.com

Published in the United States of America by
Cobb Publishing
704 E. Main
Charleston, AR 72933
CobbPublishing@gmail.com
www.CobbPublishing.com
479-747-8372

ISBN: 978-1-947622-00-5

Dedication

I am truly thankful to my God in heaven to have the opportunity
to pursue this work and to dedicate this material lovingly to my
wife, Melanie, and our four good children, Jackson, Camille,
Hannah, and Emma.
I cherish, adore, and love you all.

You are the *wealth and riches* of my life (Psalm 112:3).

Table of Contents

Part Three: Each One Reach One Bible Lessons

Introduction to the Second Edition

When I decided to write a book on church growth and personal evangelism several reasons motivated the endeavor. In the first place, I wanted to encourage God's people that the church can grow without the aid of gimmickry and compromise. In order to do this, I dedicated the first portion of the book to some general principles concerning true church growth; and not one of them includes a gimmick, a compromise, or a false doctrine. The plan is simple – go to work as faithful servants of God, work together, preach and teach the truth, and the church will grow. God will give the increase!

In the second place, I wanted to encourage brethren to go to work. But, in order for us to work to the full extent of our capabilities, we must be properly trained. It is with the goal of helping to train my brethren in personal evangelism that the second half of the book was written. In this portion of the book a personal application is made of the lessons gleaned from the first half. As the title indicates, the plan is for each one to reach one.

The Lord's church will grow in any place at any time if each one will reach one. For example, let's take a congregation that numbers 100 in attendance on Sunday morning. Of this 100, let's say seventy persons are Christians. If these seventy souls will each determine to bring one soul to Christ in the next year, in one year, the church will number at least 170 for the same services. If they teach those they have taught to do the same, in two years, they could number at least

310 for the same services. This plan will work in congregations of 20, 200, or 2,000.

With this in mind I would now like to restate a little of what I have said in the first edition of this book. Let us take the subject of church growth and personal evangelism seriously and let us study remembering that the souls of our friends, neighbors, and loved ones depend upon our obedience to the command, "Go and preach." By His spokesman Paul, God asks every generation:

"How then shall they call on him in whom they have not believed? And how shall they believe in him of whom they have not heard? And how shall they hear without a preacher?" (Romans 10:14)

If we refuse or neglect to obey Christ in the commission of His new covenant, many of our friends, neighbors, and loved ones will be eternally lost. Such neglect will also place our souls in jeopardy. The Savior has said, "Every tree that bringeth not forth good fruit is hewn down, and cast into the fire" (Matthew 7:19). We must be fruit bearing people. If we are not bringing forth fruit we are not glorifying God. Christ teaches, "Herein is my Father glorified, that ye bear much fruit; so shall ye be my disciples" (John 15:8). If we are not bringing forth fruit, we are not proving ourselves to be His disciples.

The purpose of this study is to increase biblical faithfulness. Our aim is not to challenge the Christian's biblical *faith*, but his *faithfulness* in obeying Christ's commission.

ANDY ERWIN

*All scripture references are taken from the
King James Version and
New King James Version unless otherwise noted.*

Part One: Church Growth

1
What Is Church Growth?

Church growth is a hot topic for many congregations of the Lord's church. Such an interest and desire for growth is truly encouraging. One should like to see interest and desire for growth, rather than outright apathy among his brethren, even if the desire may lack some necessary direction and vision for a time. Seemingly, most churches want to grow and most Christians want to be part of a growing church. The desire to grow must abide. Churches should be found hungering for growth.

Before we begin our study we must define our terms. What exactly is church growth? When does church growth occur? How can you know if your congregation is truly growing? Is all "growth" acceptable to God? Such answers are necessary, for many times Christians will become prematurely excited to see the attendance grow and equate that with church growth when the increase may not be growth at all.

The Scriptures teach church growth as a two-fold concept. God recognizes *spiritual growth* and *numerical growth*. God desires His church to grow both spiritually and numerically. In fact, these two aspects of church growth complement one another. Where there is spiritual growth, there will be numerical growth. When a congregation stops growing spiritually, it will stop growing numerically. Numerical growth is a fruit produced only by Christians who have first grown spiritually.

As a congregation of God's people, we should not expect numerical growth to be instantaneous. At times we can find ourselves doing all the right things to secure growth and yet be required to wait patiently for the seed to bring forth increase (see Luke 8:15). Such times should be viewed as periods of spiritual growth. Enduring faithfulness in God's wisdom will prove to be essential for church growth.

Spiritual Growth

Spiritual growth is manifested as a congregation grows *together* in the Lord. The church is the Lord's temple and we are framed together in Him. Seeing that we are framed together, we must naturally grow together.

Paul wrote of the church being "fitly framed together" and growing "unto an holy temple in the Lord. In whom ye also are builded together for an habitation of God through the Spirit" (Ephesians 2:21). Paul would also write of each member working together and complementing one another as individual joints in the grand body of Christ.

As we speak the truth in love we "grow up into him in all things, which is the head, even Christ…" Note, "From whom the whole body fitly joined together and compacted by that which every joint supplieth, according to the effectual working in the measure of every part, maketh increase of the body unto the edifying of itself in love" (Ephesians 4:15-16).

Each member of the church has been placed together to work together in the cause of Christ. We are the Lord's temple and dwelling place (1 Corinthians 3:16-17). As members of the Lord's body, we must be strong in Him. Our strength must come from Christ. We must learn to live in His strength rather than our weakness.

To grow stronger we must grow and work together. By working together we not only help one another to grow spiritually, but we also help the congregation to grow numerically.

We should also note that the church will grow spiritually by a steady diet of *feeding from the word*. Peter admonishes accordingly:

"Wherefore laying aside all malice, and all guile, and hypocrisies, and envies, and all evil speakings, As newborn babes, desire the sincere milk of the word, that ye may grow thereby: If so be ye have tasted that the Lord is gracious" (1 Peter 2:1-3).

A church that does not feed from the word regularly can never grow spiritually. The writer of Hebrews recognized a congregation that did not grow in their knowledge of the word as they should have and thus their spiritual growth was stunted.

"For when for the time ye ought to be teachers, ye have need that one teach you again which be the first principles of the oracles of God; and are become such as have need of milk, and not of strong meat" (Hebrews 5:12).

The epistle to the Hebrews was received by brethren who had wavered and grown "dull of hearing" (Hebrews 5:11). Had these brethren been growing spiritually as they should, they would not have been found guilty of being dull of hearing. Had they not been dull of hearing, they most certainly would have stood a better chance of growing spiritually.

Such dullness and density is a certain indication of spiritual immaturity. In this case, they needed to be taught again, not because they had been taught incorrectly previously, but because they were spiritually immature and did not continue in the teachings they had received. They had failed to take advantage of the opportunity to learn.

Interestingly enough, we do not read one line of scripture in Hebrews which mentions any ongoing numerical growth. It proved impossible for these brethren to grow numerically as they had become numb to the truth. Seeing that they had no interest in learning, how could they have had any interest in teaching others? If you are not excited to learn, how can you be excited to teach?

The church was failing to make any application of the gospel in their lives. Does any of this sound familiar? How does the Bible study attendance fare in your home congregation? How favorable is your own Bible study attendance and routine? How many brethren are actively and regularly teaching classes? How often do you teach Bible classes? How many sermons are you hearing on the sins of others as compared to the number of sermons that are preached on the sins of your home congregation? Is any application being made by the members from sound gospel preaching? Do brethren repent at your congregation? Are you or your brethren actively teaching in the community?

If we find ourselves answering "no" again and again, we should beware of the risk of spiritual immaturity. We must first grow spiritually before we can grow numerically. If we have no spiritual growth, we will have no numerical growth.

To grow spiritually is to grow in the grace and knowledge of the Lord. Consider Peter's final inspired written words as he "fed the sheep" before he went to be with the Lord:

"Ye therefore, beloved, seeing ye know these things before, beware lest ye also, being led away with the error of the wicked, fall from your own stedfastness. But grow in grace, and in the knowledge of our Lord and Saviour Jesus Christ. To him be glory both now and forever. Amen" (2 Peter 3:17-18).

Failing to feed from the word and failing to hunger and thirst after righteousness results in a failure to grow. Most likely, each of us understands the concept of a nutritious diet. It is not enough simply to feed at the dinner table. We must have the right diet.

It is not healthy to increase merely in size, but we want to grow in a healthy manner and into a healthy size. Likewise, we must recognize that the body of Christ must not merely feed from anything or any doctrine, but we must feed from the word of God. As there are some foods not fit for men to eat, there are some doctrines not fit, or wholesome (1 Timothy 3:6) to teach and spiritually ingest.

If our diet is from spiritually unhealthy and unwholesome words, and immature opinions, how shall we fare in our spiritual health and growth? We can neither grow spiritually or numerically without feeding upon the word of God.

Numerical Growth

Numerical growth is a concept which is easy to understand when relying solely upon the Scriptures. Numerical growth is a blessing from God and occurs only when souls are added to the church by Him (Acts 2:47). God alone adds souls to the church. He is sovereign.

By His sovereignty, God has determined that only through the preaching of the gospel will souls be called out of darkness (2 Thessalonians 2:14) and added to Christ's kingdom (Colossians 1:13) and marvelous light (1 Peter 2:9; Acts 2:38-41). Souls are added on the basis of obedience to the gospel message they have heard. Numerical growth cannot occur without the gospel being preached and obeyed.

In recent years we have seen congregations demonstrate the ability to change their teaching from the pure gospel of Christ to "another gospel" and experience an increase in attendance, but this is not church growth. How can it be growth without God? How can it be church growth if God has not given the increase?

Church growth is something done by the sovereignty of God. If you take God out of the equation, how can He add anyone to the church? How can He bless us with growth if we prohibit Him through our rebellion? God alone is the giver of increase (1 Corinthians 3:6). It is God who raises us to walk a new life (Romans 6:3-4) and forgives us of all trespasses (Colossians 2:12-13). If we dare to take Him from His throne, we forfeit any hope of being forgiven and any hope of enjoying church growth.

God must be active and the gospel must be obeyed before any congregation can grow. When man replaces the gospel with "another gospel," he is attempting to take God from His throne by exalting his own opinions above God's authority and sovereignty. Such a Christian or congregation is not serving God, but is guilty of idolizing their own hardened, opinionated hearts.

The same stand can be made against gimmickry. Gimmicks are devilish trends that come and go. To trust in gimmicks or performances is to trust in "fool's gold" rather than to "love thy [the Lord's] commandments above gold, yea, above fine gold" (Psalm 119:127).

When churches of Christ go the way of gimmicks, they find themselves in competition against the denominations on their home field. We must remove from our minds the thought of religious competition. We must not be found competing with anyone. Church growth is not a competition. Churches grow by serving God and following Christ. We must be found serving God. When we begin competing against others, we find ourselves bowing to the whims of the religious consumer rather than faithfully serving the true and living God.

Different "gospels" and performances amount to "get rich quick" schemes and should be recognized for what they are – gimmicks forged by the hands and through the fires of manmade religions. The Lord's church must remain unique and outstanding for the truth she teaches. Lost souls do not need another gimmick; they need the gospel. They do not need satisfaction polls; they need the truth. The Lord's church must be seen as the "pillar and ground" of such truth – not the source of another gimmick (1 Timothy 3:15).

Progression or Digression

Each congregation of God's people has a decision to make – shall we *progress* or *digress*? To progress is to move forward or onward. Progressing is synonymous with going forward and becoming better. How badly do you want to be a member of a congregation that is becoming better?

To digress is to turn aside from the main subject or goal. Digressing is synonymous with straying, wandering, and backing up. Honestly, does anyone want to belong to a congregation that is straying, wandering, or backing up? A church that is backing up or wandering from God's word will never be a growing church while moving in that direction.

How do we avoid such digression? First, we must remain steadfast in loving what is right. Judah fell into wayward digression when they ceased loving the truth. They were commanded:

"Obey my voice, and I will be your God, and ye shall be my people: and walk ye in all the ways that I have commanded you, that it may be well unto you" (Jeremiah 7:23).

"But they hearkened not, nor inclined their ear, but walked in the counsels and in the imagination of their evil heart, and went backward, and not forward" (Jeremiah 7:24).

In the Great Commission, the Lord gave the church a mission deserving of our love – the salvation of the human soul. The gospel is right and we must preach it to the nations.

We must also remain steadfast in denying what is evil.

"Whosoever transgresseth, and abideth not in the doctrine of Christ, hath not God. He that abideth in the doctrine of Christ, he hath both the Father and the Son. If there come any unto you, and bring not this doctrine, receive him not into your house, neither bid him God speed: For he that biddeth him God speed is partaker of his evil deeds" (2 John 9-11).

How badly do you want to have a real, rewarding relationship with God? To have this type of relationship with God we must abide in the teachings of Christ. To abide in the doctrine of Christ we must hold fast to our conviction of the gospel, rather than compromise and bid Godspeed to evil teachers. Whoever chooses to go beyond and abide not in the doctrine of Christ has not God. To follow such false teachers is to leave Christ.

In Conclusion

We have the promise of Christ's presence as we continue in His saving gospel. He will never leave or forsake us (Hebrews 13:5). Clearly, our Savior has done nothing to cause us to leave or forsake Him. The only way we will avoid digression is by allowing Christ to lead us through His word. Only Christ can lead us unto the fountains of living waters where God shall wipe away every tear from every eye.

Brethren, "Be strong and of a good courage; be not afraid, neither be thou dismayed: for the Lord thy God is with thee whithersoever thou goest" (Joshua 1:9). The faithful church will endure. The faithful church will grow. If we are faithful to the Lord, we shall grow and we shall endure!

"But they that wait upon the Lord shall renew their strength; they shall mount up with wings as eagles; they shall run, and not be weary; and they shall walk, and not faint" (Isaiah 40:31).

Discussion Questions for Chapter One

1.) Discuss the two-fold concept of church growth as discussed in this chapter.

2.) What can you do (personally) to improve spiritual growth in your life?

3.) What can you do (personally) to improve spiritual and numerical growth in your congregation?

4.) Give your thoughts on some keys to having a healthy relationship with God. How can these things help the growth of your home congregation?

2
Churches Grow When...

Churches do not grow by mistake, chance, or haphazard planning. Churches will only grow through hard work and the right mentality. As Christians, our endeavor should be to have the right mentality and the right work ethic essential for church growth.

Churches Grow When They Have...

Churches will grow best *numerically* after they have first grown *spiritually*. To grow spiritually, we must grow through adversity. Paul warned, "Yea, and all that will live godly in Christ Jesus shall suffer persecution" (2 Timothy 3:12). All who desire to live godly will face some type of adversity in this life. How we handle adversity as a congregation will determine whether or not we will grow spiritually and thus numerically.

To overcome any adversity we must remain focused and finish our course. Let us not be distracted by adversity. Even our greatest trials on this earth cannot be compared with heaven's glory. Take comfort in Paul words. He believed "that the sufferings of this present time are not worthy to be compared with the glory which shall be revealed in us" (Romans 8:18).

To grow spiritually we must grow in faith. God is with us. Therefore, "Let your conversation be without covetousness;

and be content with such things as ye have: for he hath said, I will never leave thee, nor forsake thee" (Hebrews 13:5).

Not only is God with us, but God is also for us. Let us apply Romans 8:31 to church growth: "What shall we then say to these things? If God be for us, who can be against us?"

If God has determined that His church will grow through gospel preaching and teaching, what do we have to fear or why should we hesitate to preach and teach the gospel? We must let God be glorified through the church by our strong faith (Romans 4:20)!

To grow spiritually we must grow in fellowship. Fellowship is the bond which holds us together. The church must remain together in order to grow (Ephesians 4:16). As the Savior said, "Every kingdom divided against itself is brought to desolation; and every city or house divided against itself shall not stand" (Matthew 12:25).

A strong, united congregation is an attraction to all. A congregation that is in harmony will encourage its members to invite loved ones to attend services. If the congregation is divided, embarrassed members would shun the thought of inviting even unknown citizens in the community, much less their close loved ones.

Churches Grow When They Give...

Churches grow best numerically only after they have developed a giving spirit. Perhaps the greatest need in the brotherhood is to develop a spirit always intent on truly giving God the glory.

The Lord has said, "I am the Lord: that is my name: and my glory will I not give to another, neither my praise to graven images" (Isaiah 42:8). God is not willing to share His glory and neither should His church be willing to give His glory to another. We must glorify God.

- **We glorify God by preaching His word His way.**

"If any man speak, let him speak as the oracles of God; if any man minister, let him do it as of the ability which God giveth: that God in all things may be glorified through Jesus Christ, to whom be praise and dominion for ever and ever. Amen" (1 Peter 4:11).

"But foolish and unlearned questions avoid, knowing that they do gender strife. And the servant of the Lord must not strive; but be gentle unto all men, apt to teach, patient, In meekness instructing those that oppose themselves; if God peradventure will give them repentance to the acknowledging of the truth; And that they may recover themselves out of the snare of the devil, who are taken captive by him at his will" (2 Timothy 2:23-26).

We must use our words to draw men to Jesus. Angry words and insults will not exalt Christ before men; neither will talk of sports, possessions, and careers. Certainly it is not sinful to speak of our hobbies and interests, but if we are to lift up Jesus and allow Him to draw men unto Himself, we must also speak of the One who died for us.

Have conversations about Him. Speak of Christ often in your home. Do not be as unbelievers who refuse to discuss religion. Discuss it often and lovingly. Let the world know what Jesus has done and you will be exalting Christ before men.

Let us stand where He stands. Let us praise the things He praises and condemn the things He condemns. May our words echo His words! Stand for Jesus and stand with Jesus!

Moreover, His words must become our words. If we teach our words, rather than His, we will be making disciples for ourselves rather than for Jesus. Our doctrine must ever be the Bible – the word of God. Let us defeat any and every desire to exalt our opinions, and let us fill our hearts and conversations with the word of God. We are clean through the word He spoke, not the word *we* spoke (John 15:3).

Let us invite men to return to the Bible and the Bible alone as a rule for faith and practice. Let us speak of the possibility of unity through His word. When a brother meets sorrow, let us comfort him with truth. When a soul needs saving, let us point him unto Jesus and His word. When the wayward needs restoring, let us save that soul from death by teaching him the truth of the gospel. When we do this, we lift up Jesus before men, and when they accept His truth, it is Jesus who has drawn them.

- **We must give God the glory in our Christian works.**

"Let your light so shine before men, that they may see your good works, and glorify your Father which is in heaven" (Matthew 5:16).

Our works must remain pure and undefiled (James 1:27), as they are derived from pure and undefiled hearts (Matthew 5:8).

In Luke chapter six, the Savior parallels good and evil men with good and corrupt fruit. You will know what is good by the fruit produced:

"For a good tree bringeth not forth corrupt fruit; neither doth a corrupt tree bring forth good fruit. For every tree is known by his own fruit. For of thorns men do not gather figs, nor of a bramble bush gather they grapes. A good man out of the good treasure of his heart bringeth forth that which is good; and an evil man out of the evil treasure of his heart bringeth forth that which is evil: for of the abundance of the heart his mouth speaketh. And why call ye me, Lord, Lord, and do not the things which I say?" (Luke 6:43-46)

We lift up Jesus when we serve our fellowman. True greatness is to be found in serving others. "If any man desire to be first, he shall be last of all and servant of all" (Mark 9:35).

On one occasion, the mother of James and John came with her sons, and asked for an exalted position for her sons in Christ's kingdom. She wanted either son to have a place on either side of the Lord's throne.

Jesus used this opportunity to teach her and them about true greatness, which is to be found in true service. He explained, "…whoever desires to become great among you, let him be your servant. And whoever desires to be first among you, let him be your slave – just as the Son of Man did not come to be served, but to serve, and to give His life a ransom for many" (Matthew 20:26-28; Mark 10:43-45).

- **We must glorify God when we suffer (1 Peter 4:16).**

We are called to bear the cross in suffering too. Paul said, "I bear in my body the marks of the Lord Jesus" (Galatians 6:17).

Paul's testimony of suffering is most admirable. He once wrote:

"From the Jews five times I received forty stripes minus one. Three times I was beaten with rods; once I was stoned; three times I was shipwrecked; a night and a day I have been in the deep; in journeys often, in perils of waters, in perils of robbers, in perils of my own countrymen, in perils of the Gentiles, in perils in the city, in perils in the wilderness, in perils in the sea, in perils among false brethren; in weariness and toil, in sleeplessness often, in hunger and thirst, in fastings often, in cold and nakedness." Why did he suffer so? Paul said that it was because of his "deep concern for all the churches" (2 Corinthians 11:24-28).

Paul loved the Lord and His church. He was truly vested in the mission of Christ, and if needed, he was willing to die for it. Paul understood that Jesus suffered for us and sometimes we are called to suffer for Him.

Make no mistake; the world takes notice of the manner in which Christians suffer. Non-Christians are observing and noting every time they see a Christian suffer. Will he lose his faith? How committed is he now? Does he practice what he preaches? Does he truly believe what he says?

In the case of Paul, his record bore witness of his faith. He remained faithful, dedicated, and committed to the cause of Christ even when he was made to suffer. Through each trial he exalted Christ before men and Christ used him to draw others to Him.

No other preacher has ever been as effective as Paul. Perhaps this is because Paul knew how to exalt Christ in sufferings. Paul was inspired to speak when he wrote:

"Who shall separate us from the love of Christ? Shall tribulation, or distress, or persecution, or famine, or nakedness, or peril, or sword? As it is written: 'For Your sake we are killed all day long; We are accounted as sheep for the slaughter. Yet in all these things we are more than conquerors through Him who loved us. For I am persuaded that neither death nor life, nor angels nor principalities nor powers, nor things present nor things to come, nor height nor depth, nor any other created thing, shall be able to separate us from the love of God which is in Christ Jesus our Lord" (Romans 8:35-39).

Paul had a grasp of the steadfast love of the Lord, and he presented that love to the world even in the midst of severe sufferings. Paul lifted up Christ in his life and through his life Jesus drew many souls unto Himself.

Churches Grow When They Want...

Churches grow best numerically when they want the right things. A church must want to grow, not at any cost, but in the right way. Anything worth doing is worth doing right. And, it is worth doing with all our might (Ecclesiastes 9:10)!

Churches grow the right way when they are "edified; and walking in the fear of the Lord and in the comfort of the Holy

Spirit" (Acts 9:31). The right way is the working way. Paul admonishes:

"Therefore, my beloved brethren, be ye stedfast, unmoveable, always abounding in the work of the Lord, forasmuch as ye know that your labour is not in vain in the Lord" (1 Corinthians 15:58).

Churches must not only want to grow, they must want to work. We must never become slothful. The writer of Hebrews was careful to make this point:

"And we desire that every one of you do shew the same diligence to the full assurance of hope unto the end: That ye be not slothful, but followers of them who through faith and patience inherit the promises" (Hebrews 6:11-12).

We must never give up. Again, the writer of Hebrews was careful to make this point:

"Cast not away therefore your confidence, which hath great recompence of reward. For ye have need of patience, that, after ye have done the will of God, ye might receive the promise. For yet a little while, and he that shall come will come, and will not tarry. Now the just shall live by faith: but if any man draw back, my soul shall have no pleasure in him. But we are not of them who draw back unto perdition; but of them that believe to the saving of the soul" (Hebrews 10:35-39).

Congregations of our Lord must not only want to grow, and to work, but they must also want to *remain*. A congregation should want to remain loyal to Christ.

The Ephesians had left their first love by growing disloyal to Christ. The Lord's response to these brethren proves to us who are living today that such disloyalty will not go unnoticed.

"Nevertheless I have somewhat against thee, because thou hast left thy first love... Remember therefore from whence thou art fallen, and repent, and do the first works" (Revelation 2:4, 5).

A congregation must also want to remain living. To Sardis, the Lord spoke, "I know thy works, that thou hast a name that thou livest, and art dead" (Revelation 3:1). Can you think of a more horrifying pronouncement for Christ to make unto a congregation?

Yet, speaking truthfully, every congregation is either growing or dying. To grow is to live! Anything else is certain death. When the same horrifying judgment could be said of a congregation today, the same correction must also apply: "Remember therefore how thou hast received and heard, and hold fast, and repent" (Revelation 3:3).

Churches Grow When They Reveal...

"Show us the Father," the world cries unto us. Jesus did not fail to reveal the Father to the world; and we must not fail in making God clear to men.

The world can increase in possessions, technology, and intelligence, but a world that is not thinking right about God can never be right with God. We must help the world to think right about God if we are to save them. We are called for this purpose – to increase the knowledge of God in the world.

In order for us to reveal the Father to men, He must first be revealed to us. In order for us to help others think right about God, we must first think right about Him.

God possesses certain attributes which must be understood in order for one to think right about Him. We could spend our time proving to the world the omniscience, omnipotence, and omnipresence of God. Philosophical debates of this order are centuries old.

Not to diminish these attributes of our Father, but the soul winner often has a different challenge. We are called to present other attributes of God such as grace, love, holiness, and justice.

- **Grace.**

It is not an easy task to teach of God's grace. It is not as simple as compiling references from a concordance, or definitions from a lexicon or dictionary. Perhaps we spend too much time on definitions and memorable sayings about grace.

One must look to God's encounters with man throughout the Scriptures to arrive at the whole truth on this subject. When we do so we find that grace is a primary attribute of God. Because of God's grace we can take comfort in all His other attributes – His power, His justice, His knowledge, and His holiness. And a heart that has been established by grace will share that grace; and in sharing the grace of God we will be showing the Father to the world. Through grace God saves; by grace God empowers.

- **Love.**

"God is love" (1 John 4:7). "God so loved the world…" Because He "*so* loved," He *gave*.

What could God give that would sufficiently express the depths of His love and compassion for the world? His dominion is limitless. He could choose anything or anyone. But what was the object dearest to God? What was the rarest jewel to Him? Who was it that was lying nearest to His bosom? Indeed, God looked through His vast dominions and selected His Son, His only begotten Son, and sent Him to take away the sins of the world.

The sacrifice of God's own Son is the greatest expression of His love for man that He could possibly offer. If we will only look to the cross, we will find proof of God's love for every soul. However despised or rejected a person may be, that person is the subject of God's love. When one is without a friend, a home, or even a penny to his name, that person is still the subject of God's love. No matter how lowly the individual, God loves him. No matter how perilous his life and living may be in this world, God loves him. No matter how wretched a sinner and outcast of society that person may be, because of His love, God is willing to save him.

The world needs to know the love of God and how one becomes a recipient of God's saving love. Jesus has said:

"He who has My commandments and keeps them, it is he who loves Me. And he who loves Me will be loved by My Father, and I will love him and manifest Myself to him" (John 14:21)

- **Holiness.**

God is pure holiness; and we are called to be holy because He is holy (1 Peter 1:15-16). We are representing God; but are we depicting Him accurately to the world.

Worldliness is a great problem in the Lord's church. We seem to be influenced by the world more than we are influencing the world. We can do better with God's help.

We too must be reminded of the holiness of God. We must come to see the Father as being pure holiness, so that we can reveal this aspect of Him to the lost.

God hates sin. He turns His face from such (1 Peter 3:12). We must respect the holiness of God in the way we serve Him and present ourselves before Him (Romans 12:1-2).

We realize that "God is not mocked." He is not to be trifled with. Yet, no matter how hard we may try, when we hear the angels cry "Holy, holy, holy is the Lord of hosts: the whole earth is full of His glory," all we can do is fall to our knees like Isaiah and confess "Woe is me! For I am undone…" (Isaiah 6:3, 5).

No matter how holy we attempt to live, we will sin and fall short of His glory; and this is why we must understand the biblical truth of the grace of God.

We determine to give God our very best, and yet our best will never match His glory. But, "God be thanked that while we were yet sinners, Christ died for us!"

The blood of Jesus consecrates us and makes us holy. By His blood we can have boldness to enter the holy presence of God (Hebrews 4:15-16; 10:19).

- **Justice.**

God will not acquit the wicked (Nahum 1:3). Hell exists because of the justice of God. Justice demands punishment. Satan and his angels will be punished forever. They are beyond the hope of grace.

However, this does not have to be our fate. While we deserve punishment, God's love is offering grace. He is not willing that any should perish, but that all would repent (2 Peter 3:9).

Why would anyone forsake the grace, mercy, and love of God for His justice? Yet, this is exactly what we do when we despise the spirit of grace and trample beneath our feet the blood of the Son of God (Hebrews 10:29).

- **Wisdom.**

God is all-wise. He knows what He is doing. Trust Him and "do not lean upon your own understanding." Let us do the things God has told us to do and the church will grow. It really is as simple as that.

Let us trust in God's wisdom rather than our false wisdom. He is all-wise and we are not. He has given us the plan; let us have the faith to obey it.

- **Power.**

God is all-powerful. He said He would and He will provide the increase. He holds the world in His hands. He providentially protects and guides His people. He is able to exceed all our expectations through His power (Ephesians 3:20). Why should we not trust in God for the growth of the church?

In Conclusion

Determine to grow numerically by working with the right spirit. Work together in the plan and purpose of God and do the things necessary to send His gospel light into a dark and sinful world. Only through prayer, teaching the truth, proper planning, hard work, and sacrifice will a congregation enjoy the blessing of church growth.

Little by little we may move men and draw men to Christ. It may be that a soul is drawn to Christ by a timely word spoken here and there. It may be that Christ is exalted by a kind deed of service done now and again. It could very well be that by observing the way we bear reproach for the cause of Christ, that Jesus will use these occasions to draw men unto Him.

Someday, when looking back on a life well-lived, we may be able to see the good that Jesus has done through us. Truly, "Happy is he who has the God of Jacob for his help. Whose hope is in the LORD his God" (Psalm 146:5).

"Arise, shine; for thy light is come, and the glory of the Lord is risen upon thee. For, behold, the darkness shall cover the earth, and gross darkness the people: but the Lord shall arise upon thee, and his glory shall be seen upon thee...I will glorify the house of my glory" (Isaiah 60:1-2, 7).

Discussion Questions for Chapter Two

1.) Discuss the significance of handling adversity as it pertains to church growth.

2.) Discuss the importance of glorifying God and some of the ways we can better honor Him.

3.) How do churches grow the *right* way?

4.) Do you believe your congregation is growing? If it does not grow, what will become of it? What should you be willing to do to remedy the problem?

3
Preaching that Saves

Why preach? One can preach for fame and renown. You may recall that the citizens of Babel said, "let us make a name for ourselves" (Genesis 11:4; NKJV).

A preacher may also preach with contention and strife in his heart (Philippians 1:15). He may hold to a divide and conquer agenda.

Every preacher should preach for the salvation and edification of souls. We hope this is the desire of every gospel preacher!

Preaching to Save

What was the purpose behind the preaching of the apostle Paul and the early evangelists? Paul's concern was to preach Jesus and bring people closer to salvation. Notice, "For we preach not ourselves, but Christ Jesus the Lord; and ourselves your servants for Jesus' sake" (2 Corinthians 4:5). Paul also wrote:

"To whom God would make known what is the riches of the glory of this mystery among the Gentiles; which is Christ in you, the hope of glory: Whom we preach, warning every man, and teaching every man in all wisdom; that we may present every man perfect in Christ Jesus: Whereunto I also labour, striving according to his working, which worketh in me mightily" (Colossians 1:27-29).

Preaching the Cross

Paul's agenda was put simply when he wrote, "[we] preach Christ crucified…" (1 Corinthians 1:23). Paul preached the message of the cross, and so should we. Let us preach the cross over and over again! The more firmly we can fix the cross of Christ within our hearts, the more dedicated we will be to doing His will.

The cross must be preached in order to save men from their sins. "For the preaching of the cross is to them that perish foolishness; but unto us which are saved it is the power of God" (1 Corinthians 1:18). Paul continued, "For after that in the wisdom of God the world by wisdom knew not God, it pleased God by the foolishness of preaching to save them that believe" (1 Corinthians 1:21).

We must preach Jesus! Let our brethren say, "Wonderful story of love, tell it to me again!" Herein we find the power behind gospel preaching. When souls come to understand the cross truly, and the love that placed Jesus there, they will be more likely to commit their lives to Him and win souls as well.

Preaching that Glorifies God

Preachers must preach Christ in order to glorify God. Peter wrote:

"If any man speak, let him speak as the oracles of God; if any man minister, let him do it as of the ability which God giveth: that God in all things may be glorified through Jesus Christ, to whom be praise and dominion for ever and ever. Amen" (1 Peter 4:11).

The only way a sermon will be pleasing to God is if it is the truth, the whole truth, and nothing but the truth. Seeing that His word is truth, let us preach the word of truth! The word of God must be proclaimed if preachers are to do the work of an evangelist.

"Preach the word; be instant in season, out of season; reprove, rebuke, exhort with all longsuffering and doctrine... But watch thou in all things, endure afflictions, do the work of an evangelist, make full proof of thy ministry" (2 Timothy 4:2, 5).

You will also observe that a certain element of biblical preaching can be styled "negative." Certainly it is hard to find a positive way to rebuke someone. Yet, this is what God said must be done "with all longsuffering and doctrine." Truly, this is the kind of preaching that was inspired by the Holy Spirit. Some have erred from the truth of gospel preaching believing that the Holy Spirit is against sermons which reprove and rebuke.

However, Jesus said the Comforter Himself would "reprove the world of sin, and of righteousness, and of judgment" (John 16:8). According to some, this would make the Holy Spirit a "negative" preacher!

People believe such things and express such ideas, not because of what the Bible teaches, but because that is the way *they* think it should be. But, if our preaching is to glorify God, we must go to His word and learn what *He* thinks about the subject.

Make no mistake the preacher must speak the truth in love. There is never a time to be un-Christian – especially in the pulpit. Thus, the preacher must learn to speak on very difficult and controversial subjects while having his speech seasoned with grace.

The point we are making is this: he must preach the word. This may mean that he should "warn everyone night and day with tears." This may mean that he must deal with worldliness in the church. Preaching the word may also mean that he must educate the church on such matters and grace and forgiveness. Whatever the subject, the preacher has a textbook which he must use if he is to please and glorify God – the Holy Bible.

Preaching the Will of God

Every preacher must submit his will to the will of God. "Let Thy will be done." As God said to Jonah, He says to preachers today, "Preach the preaching that I bid thee."

We must humble ourselves and exalt our God. How can one say that his preaching exalts God, if God's will on the subject is not taught? Obviously, we must preach the will and word of God.

Let us return to the fundamentals of church growth. The Lord's church grows when (1) the gospel is preached by the Christian; (2) the gospel is obeyed by the sinner; (3) the Lord forgives that person and adds the now saved one to His church (Acts 2:47). Thus, we find that the church will never truthfully grow unless the gospel is preached and obeyed. Our opinions will not get the job done. The doctrines and commandments of men will not get the job done. Jokes and personal antidotes will not do the job. We must preach the gospel! We must preach Jesus!

Our sermons must be aimed at drawing people nearer to God by preaching the truth as it is in Jesus, for this is the will of God. Warning, rebuking when necessary, always speaking the truth in love, let preachers speak the oracles of almighty God.

Preaching the Truth in Love

In Ephesians 4:11-16 we read instructions given to the church pertaining to their spiritual growth. From the immediate context the following points are clear: Paul was concerned with the perfecting of the saints, which is also the edifying of the body. To perfect the saints is to edify the body, as both terms are synonymous and pertain to spiritual maturity.

Paul was also concerned with the unity of the faith that is based upon knowledge. He understood that such knowledge came by teaching and therefore warned the church not to be tossed to and fro by every wind of doctrine – which of course means teaching, and in this case, false teaching.

To keep from being overcome by every wind of doctrine, we must speak the truth in love. Herein, Paul teaches us how the church is to be edified unto a perfect man; that is, by the preaching of the truth. The prepositional phrase "in love" is restated when we are told that the "increase of the body" (that is the spiritual growth and maturity of the church) is done "unto the edifying of itself in love."

Love is undoubtedly the motivating factor for Paul's words and should be the motivating factor within the church. Ultimately it is love that will lead to our spiritual growth, numerical growth, maturity, and unity. Love must be the motivating factor for all that we do or say.

Some members of the body of Christ have been convinced that "hard preaching" is the antithesis to speaking the truth in love. If this is truly the case Jesus would be guilty of not speaking the truth in love, for He taught hard sayings (John 6:60). People quit following the Lord because of His hard preaching (v.66).

Let us also look to Paul, the man who wrote the saying under consideration. He was a hard preacher and admonished Timothy to be the same. He warned that the time would come "when they will not endure sound doctrine; but after their own lusts shall they heap to themselves teachers, having itching ears; And they shall turn away their ears from the truth, and shall be turned unto fables" (2 Timothy 4:3-4).

Faithfully preaching the gospel requires that we preach difficult sermons at difficult times. However, one can preach a hard sermon and speak the truth in love, if love is truly the reason for the sermon.

Preachers are often instructed to avoid any message of rebuke. It is believed that such a message is too "negative" and not conducive to speaking the truth in love. Accordingly, if preachers are to speak the truth in love, we are told that we must avoid rebuking people who are living in sin. We are told that speaking the truth in love is purely positive in its nature.

However, God Himself loves those whom He rebukes and chastens (Hebrews 12:5-6). God is love (1 John 4:16) and God rebukes and chastens.

Some people can be saved with compassion. Other people must be saved with fear (Jude 22). Paul said, "…knowing therefore the terror of the Lord, we persuade men" (2 Corinthians 5:11). Paul persuaded men by the terror of the Lord because he loved their souls. He was speaking the truth in love. To the Corinthians, whom Paul loved very much, he warned that he might have to come unto them with "sharpness" if they did not repent of certain sins, including suffering false teachers (2 Corinthians 13:10). Thus a "negative sermon" may indeed be preached and the truth be spoken in love.

Many preachers of today have decided that the solution for preaching hard sermons while speaking the truth in love is to preach with more "balance." In other words, preach hard lessons when you must, but do not do it too often.

It is certainly wise for a preacher to provide a healthy diet of the meat and milk of the word (Hebrews 5:12). A preacher must also use good judgment in the assortment of sermons he selects – from subject to style. However, as preachers, we must keep in mind that in some congregations certain sins need to be treated more aggressively than in other congregations. To avoid teaching such difficult lessons for fear of doing it too often is neither balanced nor faithful.

At times a gospel preacher may spend more time and energy trying to teach his congregation about a specific sin than otherwise he would. Is he not speaking the truth in love because of the amount of time he spends trying to help them understand truth? Again we must see that as long as love is the motivating factor for what he does (assuming he is in fact preaching the truth) he will be speaking the truth in love.

On the other hand, some preachers seem overjoyed at the prospect of preaching a hard sermon. For them, it is an opportunity to prove to the audience that they are "sound," or to make a name for being sound. Such preachers equate sensitivity with being unsound. Of course this would render Jeremiah as being unsound (Lamentations 3:48).

It seems that both the one who refuses to preach a hard lesson for fear of loss, and the other who seizes the opportunity with the hope of gain are preaching for selfish ambition (Philippians 1:16, NKJV). In either case, love is not their motivation, but personal gain.

It has become common to hear of preachers using more of a story-telling form of sermon, rather than a sermon filled with book, chapter, and verse, believing this is the way to speak the truth in love.

Paul warned that brethren would be turned from sound teaching unto fables (2 Timothy 4:4). A fable is a myth, legend, or tale. According to *Thayer's Greek-English Lexicon*, a fable can be a narrative story whether true or false. We must, however, be very careful in this accusation. Our Lord spoke by parables to illustrate a deeper spiritual meaning, but there was a deeper spiritual meaning. He did not tell stories merely for the sake of avoiding hard preaching, or saying something that might offend. He used parables as a teaching tool to get to the meat of the word. Such must be the case in our use of narratives.

Let us not make speaking the truth in love harder than it has to be. The truth can and must be spoken in love when our hearts are truly interested in the eternal welfare of the individuals we are teaching. Let us keep the souls of men in mind, eternity in view, and God's word in our hearts, and we will have no problem speaking the truth in love.

In Conclusion

Many years ago the venerable Cled E. Wallace wrote the following:

"Much is being said about the right kind of preaching and writing. Charges of 'hard' and 'soft' are being bandied back and forth. With as plain a book as the New Testament in hand, and with its abundant supply of examples of the very best preaching and writing, it ought not to be a difficult thing to determine the kind of both that should be done. A direct appeal to the New Testament, its preachers and its writers, ought to settle any question that arises in such a connection. Men who say the most about 'the right method of approach,' 'constructive articles,' etc., betray the fact that a lot of their ideas come from modern psychology, materialistic philosophy, and sectarian sources rather than from Jesus and the apostles. It is futile to do a lot of talking about the method of approach, when you never approach. It would improve some preachers and writers if they could forget about the method and go ahead and approach. The main idea is getting there anyhow" (Cled E. Wallace, *Bible Banner*, Vol. 1, Num. 11, June 1939).

As you can see, this article was written in June of 1939, and it is as timely as ever. In fact, quite a few brethren continue to rely upon "modern psychology, materialistic philosophy, and sectarian sources rather than from Jesus and the apostles" when it comes to their method of preaching. They hide behind their false conception of Paul's charge to "speak the truth in love" while disregarding the divinely recorded sermons he preached. If one desires to know what Paul meant when he told us to speak the truth in love, go to the examples of his sermons and see how he did it. Moreover, go and learn from the sermons preached by the apostles, Stephen, and our Lord Himself.

In these words of encouragement to Timothy, Paul defines the subject of biblical preaching:

"Preach the word! Be ready in season and out of season. Convince, rebuke, exhort, with all longsuffering and teaching" (2 Timothy 4:2; NKJV).

➤ Biblical preaching demands preaching the word – whether it is popular or not.

➢ Biblical preaching requires preaching doctrine or "teaching" in a way that will "convince, rebuke, and exhort" the hearer.

➢ Biblical preaching appeals to the spiritual as well as the intellectual nature of man. It requires the whole of God's word being imparted to the whole of man.

Through biblical preaching, we address the intellect, awaken the spirit, and appeal to the will of the listener. We encourage those listening to be "doers of the word and not hearers only" (James 1:22). We expect them to respond faithfully to the message, but we should avoid gauging our success on the basis of their response. We must "preach the word" regardless of how God's divine truth may be received by our fellow-man. The people must know that their preacher loves them; but they must also know that he loves God *more*.

Biblical preaching is not just a matter of style, taste, or preference. Whether or not one preaches the word of God is a matter of authority. That which distinguishes the message of the gospel preacher from the message of the world is the authority by which the message is spoken. Biblical preaching is a message authorized by God (cf. Titus 2:15). It is the only message authorized by God, as it is the word of God.

Biblical preaching is intended to save man from his sins, but it will not always be pleasing to man. For this very reason, preachers of the gospel and their families must be more concerned with the salvation of souls than job security. Preachers who are more concerned with job security than the salvation of souls need to repent or get out of the way. If a man is ministering only to his personal self-interests and job security, he is doing nothing more than "peddling the word" (2 Corinthians 2:17), "exploiting with deceptive words" (2 Peter 2:3), in order to receive "wages of unrighteousness" (2 Peter 2:13).

A gospel preacher should never be concerned with being the most popular speaker in town or speaking only that with which the majority agrees. Anyone can do that. But, it takes a gospel preacher to preach the word – in season and out of season – and to return our communities, our churches, and our families to God.

An entire generation (or two) has been convinced that the church will not grow unless the gospel is preached in a "positive" way. Of course, the critics determine what is positive and what is negative. "O' Ye of little faith." Just preach the word!

One may wonder why we have been so forthright in this chapter. We have done so because preaching is important to God. And, if it is important to God, it should be important to us. I was taught early on that "God had but one Son, and He made Him a preacher." Let us preach God's word God's way, and we will see the Lord's church grow as a result. Sow and water and let God give the increase!

"For do I now persuade men, or God? or do I seek to please men? for if I yet pleased men, I should not be the servant of Christ" (Galatians 1:10).

Discussion Questions for Chapter Three

1.) Why is biblical preaching essential to church growth?

2.) Can biblical preaching be "negative" at times? Can such a sermon still be preached in love?

3.) What will be the benefit of preaching the message of the cross for the church and those who hear such sermons?

4.) Why should this subject be important to us?

4

God Gives the Increase

Let's begin this chapter by stating a few facts upon which we base our conviction for church growth.

➤ Church growth is a spiritual blessing given by the hand of almighty God.

➤ Spiritual blessings are conditioned upon man's obedience to Christ (Ephesians 1:3).

➤ Christ has stipulated two conditions for church growth – sowing and watering the seed of the kingdom (1 Corinthians 3:6).

➤ If a congregation will meet these conditions, God will bless their efforts.

➤ If we sow and water, God will give the increase (1 Corinthians 3:6-7).

➤ If we remain faithful to God, our blessings will come from Him.

➤ Only when these conditions are obeyed is our Father in heaven glorified by our labors.

Do you agree with these statements? Have you put your faith in God's plan for church growth?

Are You Sowing the Seed of the Kingdom, Brother?

What is involved in sowing the seed of the kingdom? First, we must have the right seed. The word of God is the right seed. God's word is the seed of the kingdom (Luke 8:11). It is incorruptible and enduring forever (1 Peter 1:23).

God has afore ordained that every fruit yielding seed is to bring forth its fruit after its own kind (Genesis 1:12). Therefore, the only seed that we can sow that will bring a soul into the kingdom is the word of God, the seed of the kingdom (Colossians 1:13; 2 Thessalonians 2:14).

One cannot sow a tradition which takes man away from God (Matthew 15:8), makes void the word of God (Mark 7:13), and will be rooted up in the last day by God (Matthew 15:13), into the human heart and expect a Christian to be born. It cannot happen. Manmade traditions are different seeds altogether. In order for a Christian to be born, the seed of the kingdom – the word of God – must be planted and watered in a person's heart. God has revealed no other way.

Secondly, we must have faith in the product. Why bother sowing a seed for which you have no faith? Why bother teaching the word of God if you do not believe it can still prick a person's heart? We must have faith that the word of the Lord has not run its course, that it is not outdated, and that it lives and abides forever. We must believe that the gospel can still influence the human spirit even as it did our own.

Thirdly, we must sow the seed. The word of God is living, active, abiding, and enduring forever (Hebrews 4:12; 1 Peter 1:23). We must not stop at merely believing in the power of the word. We must preach the powerful gospel (Romans 1:15-16)!

A person can have the best corn seed available, but until he plants the seed in the ground he should not expect any harvest. Would that person not look silly standing in the middle of his garden, scratching his head, wondering why his crop has failed all while the seed remained sitting on the shelf?

Sow the seed *first*, and then enjoy the harvest. So it is with the word of God. The word engrafted surely has no equal. If the Bible is taught, souls will be saved (James 1:21). But, until it is sown into human hearts, we should not expect a thing!

Is the Seed You've Planted Getting Enough Water?

Watering is tending to the sown seed. To water is to go back and care for that seed which was sown. The seed must have water to grow. Sow with care and water with hope and love.

The Scriptures instruct us in the need to love and continue loving the lost soul. To love is to continue caring through prayer, teaching, visiting, or whatever kindness we could properly bestow. The only way to water the seed is to keep teaching the word of God by precept and by setting the right example (see Philippians 4:9).

We must use the word of God for our seed and our water. The word of God is the water of life (Revelation 22:17). To go back and water with a manmade doctrine is to wait on a cloud with no water (Jude 12). To rely on the words of men is to trust in a broken cistern (Jeremiah 2:13).

Why sow the seed only to be careless in watering? Yet, fearfully we acknowledge the many souls who are now perishing under scorching temptations because of our failure to continue caring for them and teaching them as we should have done. We must continue teaching.

Sow and water – these are the conditions. By trusting in the word of God we will have the right seed and the necessary water to secure a bountiful harvest.

How Can I Know the Gospel Will Work?

We hold the same assurance for church growth as we hold for God forgiving and continuing to forgive our sins (Colossians 2:13; 1 John 1:9), granting us an everlasting inheritance (Ephesians 1:18), and hearing and answering our prayers (1 Peter 3:12; Ephesians 3:12; Hebrews 4:16). If we can trust God to forgive us, keep His promise of our inheritance and answer our prayers, can we not trust Him to bless our labors in His kingdom?

Have we fully committed our trust to God? Do we trust in His grace as we should? Have we found the necessary peace and assurance that comes by knowing that our labor is not in vain in the Lord (1 Corinthians 15:58)?

Patience (or endurance) is needed when sowing the seed (Luke 8:15). We cannot give up on the process if we are not seeing immediate results. Sometimes we need to sow the seed again in the same spot. Sometimes we need to till the ground again. But, the fact remains: you must have seed; you must plant that seed; you must water that seed; and you must give the seed time to grow. "And let us not be weary in well doing: for in due season we shall reap, if we faint not" (Galatians 6:9).

What if we are seeing no increase of either a spiritual or numerical nature? Something is evidently wrong, right? Before assigning blame, losing faith, or becoming too discouraged let us first ask, are we truly sowing and watering the seed of the kingdom? How hard are we working to do our part in the church growth process? There are no shortcuts to take. We must patiently keep His word, do His will, and wait for the Father's promised harvest. As we have said before, anything worth doing is worth doing right, and it is worth doing with all our might.

A Tale of Two Churches

Allow me to illustrate what we are discussing with "a tale of two churches." At one time in this country, the Lord's church grew simply by being faithful to God. Brethren believed God would provide the increase – and grow they did! Revival swept the cities and plains and souls were added to the Lord in such vast numbers that all religions took note and hated the growing band of faithful Christians.

However, it was not long until Satan determined to destroy this church much like he tried to do in Jerusalem (Acts 2-12). He did so by convincing some brethren that they needed to take church growth into their own hands and add various elements to their worship and doctrines not found in the New

Testament. They did so believing the church must compromise with the world in order to grow. They had lost sight of the reason for their success.

Satan convinced most of these brethren to follow this line of false reasoning. The remnant attempted to remain faithful to the New Testament in their preaching and practice. They did so believing God would still provide the increase and bless their efforts to sow and water the seed of the kingdom. The fundamental difference in these ideals led to division and two churches existing where once there was one.

The progressive movement, as it would soon be designated, was immediately resisted by faithful Christians. Yet, the damage was being done wherever the progressives could teach and persuade men to accept their view of the spirit of the law. Many of the congregations north of the Ohio River accepted these views, as this area was heavily saturated by a paper ironically known as the *Christian Standard.*

According to a government religious census in 1906, the combined number of the two groups was 1,142,359 members in 10,942 congregations. Of this number, 982,701 members in 8,293 churches would call themselves the Christian Church or Disciples, while only 159,685 members in 2,649 congregations would be known as the churches of Christ. Of course these are manmade statistics, and only God knows the true numbers.

By the time of the 1926 census there would be an estimated 433,714 members and 6,226 local churches of Christ. From the time of the 1906 census to the 1926 census, the churches of Christ grew by an estimated 274,056 members and 3,577 congregations.

Accordingly, the increase of individual membership was 171% and 135% for congregations. That period marked the most phenomenal period of growth by percentage for the churches of Christ in the Twentieth Century. The church outgrew the nation, even as the nation grew very well (38% from 1906-1926).

How did the Christian Church fair during this period? In 1902, they decided to join Protestant churches in the "Federation of Churches and Church Workers." By so doing, they stated their desire to be one of the denominations. The plea to come out of denominationalism had been lost to them forever.

In 1909, a Centennial Convention was held by the Disciples in Pittsburg, Pennsylvania. During this affair, Samuel Hardin (grandson of Barton W. Stone) attacked the old-time beliefs of the brethren, repudiated the Virgin Birth, and stated that baptism should be dispensed with and all denominations should be accepted without it. It is said that the chairman could scarcely quiet the crowd of protestors.

By 1912, at the International Convention of Disciples of Christ which met in Louisville, Kentucky, the Disciples' leaders decided to establish a delegated central organization to manage and control their denomination.

While the Lord did indeed give the increase to those who remained faithful, the Christian Church would again split. A group known as Disciples of Christ emerged. It is a group which now stands for nothing. It is believed that no other denomination lost more members by percentage than did this group in the Twentieth Century.

They believed the way to grow was to compromise with the world. They were wrong. By befriending the world, they became an enemy to God (James 4:4). God provides no increase to those who oppose His word.

Just as a tale of two churches was written in the Twentieth Century, it seems that another tale of two churches will be written in the Twenty-First Century. Lord willing, what will be said of our generation 100 years from now?

Undoubtedly, the brethren of 1900 were discouraged and disappointed by the digression of their brethren. It would have been easy for them to allow their frustrations and disappointments to overrule their better judgment. Thankfully, they resolved never to quit, never to give in, and never to give up! As a result, they launched the church into a period of unprecedented growth. Where would the churches of Christ be today without this outstanding generation of brethren?

What shall be our resolve? What shall be our legacy? Will we leave the Lord's church in a better condition than we found it? Will we move beyond the division of a past generation and help the church to grow once again?

We must never lose sight of that great plea which calls for men and women to abandon every creed and church not found in the Scriptures and to return to the ancient faith which was once for all delivered to the saints (Jude 3).

In Conclusion

Evangelistic churches grow both spiritually and numerically. Satan would love nothing more than to see congregations lose sight of the importance of evangelism and to lose sight of the true nature of undenominational Christianity. He would love to see us become distracted or preoccupied with other things of lesser importance. In many cases, he has done his job and we have let him.

It is time that we let God do His job! God will provide the increase. God wants His church to grow. He is not willing that any should perish. We too must not be willing for any to perish. God would have all men come to knowledge of the truth. We must have the same attitude as our Father, and do all we can to bring the truth to the lost.

The things which are important to God must be important to us. As our Savior put all of His trust in His Father, so too must we. Allow God to give the increase. Trust in Him and His plan to save the lost. Let us be laborers together with God. Only then will God give the increase.

"And let us not be weary in well doing: for in due season we shall reap, if we faint not" (Galatians 6:9).

Discussion Questions for Chapter Four

1.) What are the conditions or commandments for church growth?

2.) Will God give the increase if we choose not to sow and water the seed?

3.) If it is possible for the kingdom to grow without sowing and watering the seed of the kingdom, please list other examples in God's creation of things that can grow on their own without a seed first being planted?

4.) What has recent history taught us concerning doctrinal compromise and true church growth?

5
Love Manifested Wins Souls

Love is the greatest emotion the soul can enjoy (1 Corinthians 13:13). To love is to be like God, for God is love. To love is to be born of God.

"Beloved, let us love one another: for love is of God; and every one that loveth is born of God, and knoweth God. He that loveth not knoweth not God; for God is love" (1 John 4:7-8).

John further wrote, "And we have known and believed the love that God hath to us. God is love; and he that dwelleth in love dwelleth in God, and God in him" (1 John 4:16).

We must learn what love is and how to love truly as it pleases God. Love "abides forever" (1 Corinthians 13:8). If we are to abide forever with God in heaven we must first learn of love and how to love.

In this chapter we will be discussing the pivotal role love has in the growth of the Lord's church. Let us note four ways our love is to be manifested and what this means.

Let Us Love God

We must love the Lord. Jesus taught, "Thou shalt love the Lord thy God with all thy heart, and with all thy soul, and with all thy mind. This is the first and great commandment" (Matthew 22:37-38).

55

Our love for the Lord must be without equal. The Savior would teach this even as it pertains to our family ties. Observe:

"He that loveth father or mother more than me is not worthy of me: and he that loveth son or daughter more than me is not worthy of me. And he that taketh not his cross, and followeth after me, is not worthy of me. He that findeth his life shall lose it: and he that loseth his life for my sake shall find it" (Matthew 10:37-38).

The truth expressed in this passage is important to note in the context of church growth because churches tend to become family-oriented. Some congregations can even become "family owned and operated."

The danger in such a development is that they cease to become God-oriented for the sake of the family. Elders are appointed, not because they meet the qualifications set forth by God, but because they serve as a delegate for a particular family. The work of the congregation can tend to center around the desire of the family. The choice of who is to preach and what is to be preached is also determined by the family. Church discipline upon sinning family members is avoided. On and on we could go with other examples of the danger of being family-oriented instead of God-oriented.

Whenever a congregation takes its focus off of saving souls and places it upon anything else, bad things happen. Anytime a congregation decides to "love these more than Me" bad things will happen. But, if we truly love the Lord and seek to serve Him above all others, the church will grow.

Sometimes the truth hurts. Those who teach the truth will always be deemed to be hateful by those who hate the truth. However, this is not necessarily the case. Many times a gospel preacher will teach a lesson on a very difficult subject which affects many people he loves. He does so, not because he hates these people, but because he loves them and wishes for them to be forgiven through their repentance.

Nevertheless, truth can be controversial – especially for those who do not want to believe it. Christ warned accordingly:

"Suppose ye that I am come to give peace on earth? I tell you, Nay; but rather division: For from henceforth there shall be five in one house divided, three against two, and two against three. The father shall be divided against the son, and the son against the father; the mother against the daughter, and the daughter against the mother; the mother in law against her daughter in law, and the daughter in law against her mother in law" (Luke 12:51-53).

Standing for the truth will bring persecution upon us even from our own families. Such persecution is not because we have done something wrong in choosing to love and obey God above all others, but it is because those who are "of the world" do not know Jesus. Our love for God above all others will be tested in our willingness to endure persecutions, even if it comes from those closest to us.

"And the brother shall deliver up the brother to death, and the father the child: and the children shall rise up against their parents, and cause them to be put to death. And ye shall be hated of all men for my name's sake: but he that endureth to the end shall be saved" (Matthew 10:21-22).

A Christian's love for God must become the most important aspect of life. Such a love for God will lead us to endure the controversy and persecution we must suffer for believing and teaching the truth.

To love God is to keep His word. "And this is love, that we walk after his commandments…" (2 John 6). John would also write:

"By this we know that we love the children of God, when we love God, and keep his commandments. For this is the love of God, that we keep his commandments: and his commandments are not grievous" (1 John 5:2-3).

By keeping His word we manifest our love for Him. Christ said, "If ye love me, keep my commandments" (John 14:15). The Savior taught His disciples:

"As the Father hath loved me, so have I loved you: continue ye in my love. If ye keep my commandments, ye shall abide in my love; even as I have kept my Father's commandments, and abide in his love" (John 15:9-11).

We manifest our love for God by doing the works He has commanded. We are His "workmanship created unto good works" (Ephesians 2:10). Our labor for the Lord is a "labor of love" (1Thessalonians 1:3; Hebrews 6:10). Paul challenged Corinth to "prove the sincerity of your love" by giving a generous collection unto the suffering church at Jerusalem (2 Corinthians 8:8).

Our love for the Lord will also keep us waiting and watching for His return (2 Thessalonians 3:5; Matthew 24:42-44). "Tares" are sown when we sleep on the job (Matthew 13:25). Brethren among us who are asleep must "Awake...and arise from the dead, and Christ shall give thee light" (Ephesians 5:14).

Let Us Love the Church

"Let brotherly love continue" (Hebrews 13:1). May we never become church slappers! Let us love the church and realize how precious we are to Christ.

Our Lord has given us an example of brotherly love:

> ➤ "love one another, as I have loved you" (John 15:12);

> ➤ "forgive one another as God in Christ has forgiven you" (Ephesians 4:31-32);

> ➤ "let this mind be in you, which was also in Christ Jesus" (Philippians 2:5-8).

Our love for the church must also be in *purity* of heart:

"Seeing ye have purified your souls in obeying the truth through the spirit unto unfeigned love of the brethren, see that ye love one another with a pure heart fervently" (1 Peter 1:22).

Our love for the church should also be with *piety* of heart.

"If there be therefore any consolation in Christ, if any comfort of love, if any fellowship of the Spirit, if any bowels and mercies, Fulfill ye my joy, that ye be likeminded, having the same love, being of one accord, of one mind. Let nothing be done through strife or vainglory; but in lowliness of mind let each esteem other better than themselves. Look not every man on his own things, but every man also on the things of others" (Philippians 2:1-4).

Let Us Love Souls

"Thou shalt love thy neighbor as thyself" (Matthew 22:39). The church must love souls in order to grow. Everyone has a soul (1 Thessalonians 5:23); everyone will live somewhere forever (Ecclesiastes 12:7; Hebrews 9:27; John 5:28-29); and everyone is important to God (Hebrews 2:9).

God is not willing that anyone should perish (2 Peter 3:9) and in love has offered His Son as a Savior for all men (1 Timothy 4:10; 1 John 4:10). Seeing that we are the church of God (Acts 20:28), how devoted to the salvation of lost souls ought we to be?

Love that pleases God is a selfless love. It is love that will cause us to put God first and commit ourselves to serving Him and our fellow man. As we have stated previously, when we lose sight of saving souls, bad things will happen. Churches that put other things ahead of the mission God has given them tend to:

➢ Argue over the building and grounds;

➢ Hoard money in the treasury;

➢ Have discord in the eldership;

- ➢ Have elders which oversee the building and treasury rather than shepherding the souls of the congregation;

- ➢ Have discord with the preacher;

- ➢ Complain about the deacons;

- ➢ Complain about youth activities (or lack thereof)

- ➢ Murmur incessantly about anything and everything that does not go to suit them.

A church like this will never grow and will never reach its full potential. It is too busy worrying about getting its way and shows very little concern for God's way and God's mission. As a result, souls in that community will march into eternity, without as much as a passing glance. Brethren, if this is the case in your home congregation, this must change.

Let Us Love Self

The Lord was not advocating the selfishness we just described when He said "love your neighbor as *yourself*" but naturally there must be a wholesome love for our self and our own eternal wellbeing.

God loves us (1 John 4:9, 19); He knows we can faithfully serve Him (1 Corinthians 10:13); and He wants to spend eternity with us (John 3:16). Therefore, there must be something special and worthy about us if God loves us and God sees our potential.

Our Heavenly Father is not going to desire anything of us that we are unable to do. Let us be confident to do the work! Let us be confident that we can do the will of God. "Be thou strong and very courageous!" "Be strong in the Lord and the power of His might!" Live in His strength rather than your weakness.

Whatever our station is in life, whether we are bricklayers or stay-at-home moms, we must be of the disposition to teach and share Christ with those who are among us. Do not be afraid, but exhibit the spirit "of power, love, and of a sound mind" that God has given you.

Have confidence in yourself that you can make a difference in this world one soul at a time. This is not a haughty spirit, but a spirit that believes you can do whatsoever the Lord has commanded.

Let Us Love Truth

The Lord's church has the truth; but do we love it enough to teach it? Indeed, if it could be said that something is lacking from among God's people today, one could reasonably claim that we are missing the element of boldness which is fundamental to saving a lost and dying world.

As with Joshua in the days of old, we too must "Be strong and of a good courage; be not afraid, neither be thou dismayed: for the LORD thy God is with thee whithersoever thou goest" (Joshua 1:9).

♦ Pray for boldness.

The church in Jerusalem prayed that they could speak with boldness (Acts 4:29) and they did (v.31). Paul asked for prayers that he could boldly teach and preach the word of God (Ephesians 6:19-20, Philippians 1:20), which he did.

♦ Study, Study, STUDY!

As we learn the truth and know the truth (John 8:32), we will be more confident to teach the truth. Paul was not ashamed of the gospel because he knew what it was, and that he was in fact preaching the truth (Romans 1:16 ff.).

♦ Place fear in its proper place.

So many times we do nothing because we are afraid of making a mistake, or losing a friend. "But and if ye suffer for righteousness' sake, happy are ye: and be not afraid of their terror, neither be troubled" (1 Peter 3:14). Rather than being troubled by what people might do or say, Peter teaches, "But sanctify the Lord God in your hearts: and be ready always to give an answer to every man that asketh you a reason of the hope that is in you with meekness and fear" (v.15).

Ezekiel was due to face his critics. And the Lord told him not to be afraid of their words or dismayed at their looks (2:6), but to listen to Him and speak His word (v.7). The only One we need to fear is God (Matthew 10:26-28).

♦ Remember that we will face the Lord in judgment and give an answer for what we did and did not do (James 4:17).

Paul could truthfully say that he was free from the blood of all men because he had the boldness to preach the whole counsel of God (Acts 20:26-27). Can we say the same?

♦ Refrain from criticizing your brethren who have the courage to teach the truth boldly.

Oftentimes, we are our worst enemy in this regard. Do you find it interesting how some of our brethren are willing to rebuke the one who has boldness and cares enough to correct the erring brother, but will not rebuke the soul bringing shame and reproach upon the church? They are bold enough to criticize the person who is attempting to do the right thing, but cowardly shrink away from doing the right thing themselves. This too must change.

When we act this way, we "strain out the gnat and swallow the camel" (Matthew 23:24). Moreover, when we act this way we discourage our brethren who have boldness, rather than encourage them to use their boldness as a blessing – and we wonder why we are not growing!

♦   Dispel the notion that boldness is ugliness.

While one can be bold to a fault, it is not necessarily true that all bold speech is ugliness. Certainly our Lord was not being ugly when He was speaking boldly. Boldness does not have to be ugliness. Boldness, as we see it, is having the courage to teach the truth when it is most needed.

Brethren who are bold need to be careful to season their speech with grace when necessary (Colossians 4:6). Give your critics nothing to criticize. Yet, if they persist in their criticisms, "Be strong and of a good courage" (Joshua 1:6), for you are doing the right thing by speaking the truth in love in times of great need and eternal significance.

Draw strength from others who are bold in the truth. Paul's example even in spite of suffering helped others to speak the word with boldness (see Philippians 1:14). We can do the same by setting such an example today. The worst mistake we can make is to do nothing at all. None of us wants to go to the final judgment with blood on our hands because we were too afraid to speak the truth. Let us have the courage to obey the Lord, and the boldness to speak the truth.

In Conclusion

Has love been made perfect in us? John has instructed how we might have this perfect love:

"And we have known and believed the love that God hath to us. God is love; and he that dwelleth in love dwelleth in God, and God in him. Herein is our love made perfect, that we may have boldness in the day of judgment: because as he is, so are we in this world" (1 John 4:16-17).

We must dwell in God, having a personal communion with him, as God is love. We must walk in His light (1 John 1:7). As Philip said to Jesus, "Show us the Father" so too does the world say to us "Show us the Father." Let us show the world the love of God that lives and abides in us.

A perfect love will cause the Lord's church to grow. Such love will give us boldness and assurance as we look toward a never ending eternity as faithful children of God, rejoicing evermore, having accepted heaven's commission.

"And the Spirit and the bride say, Come. And let him that heareth say, Come. And let him that is athirst come. And whosoever will, let him take the water of life freely" (Revelation 22:17).

Discussion Questions for Chapter Five

1.) Discuss the importance of putting God first.

2.) How does the mission of saving souls compare with the other objectives in your home congregation and in your life personally?

3.) Discuss the value of having boldness in soul winning.

4.) Discuss ways in which true love will affect the growth of your home congregation.

6
What the Church Needs Now

A well-known song melodiously begins, "What the world needs now is love, sweet love." Indeed the world needs love. God is love; and if the world is to love truly and be saved, the world must receive God.

To receive God is to yield to the word of God. For the world to yield to God, and therefore to love, the church must fulfill its solemn and sacred responsibility. God is sending us into the world so that the world might know and understand His love.

For the people of this world to yield and thus receive God, we must convince them of the need to obey God. Paul said, "Knowing therefore the terror of the Lord, we persuade men…" (2 Corinthians 5:11). Sinners in the world must learn and be faced with the fact that they are lost. They must also learn that God cares. The goodness of the Lord will lead them to repentance (Romans 2:4).

What the world needs now is for Christians to be ready and willing to share the gospel of salvation. The world needs hope that can only come from a message of hope.

Seeing that we have stated a few needs of the world, what if we were to write a song entitled, "What the Church Needs Now?" What do you suppose we could say?

Renewed Hope

In the next two chapters we are going to be addressing the attitudes of optimism and pessimism and the ways in which each attitude can affect the growth of the church. Optimism is at the heart of the gospel. The gospel tells us good will overcome evil. Good will prevail. God will prevail! If we are on the Lord's side, we will prevail. Therefore, the church can and will make a difference in this world as long as we are faithful to God. Just as Joshua was promised that he could take the land if he remained faithful to the Lord, we can take the land for Christ if we will only remain true to Him.

Yet, in many places, the church needs a renewed hope, or in the biblical sense of the word, *expectation*. In sports, championship teams *expect* to win. We must expect to make a difference in the world with the gospel. We should be shocked when the gospel is not believed and obeyed, rather than when it is obeyed.

If Joshua did not truly expect to take the Land of Promise, he never would have attempted the first battle. If we don't expect to save souls then why would we bother? Perhaps this is why some of us do not bother to try.

What does the church need most in order to increase our hope as the children of God? We need Christ. We need to refocus on Jesus. We need to refocus on the importance of our mission. We need to refocus on the Savior who is on our side. "For consider him that endured such contradiction of sinners against himself, lest ye be wearied and faint in your minds" (Hebrews 12:3).

Jesus knew He was not going to be left in the grave. He knew His church would be established. He also knew it would begin as a mustard seed and grow to the point of lodging all the birds of the air (Matthew 13:31-32).

What do we *know* about the church? We know that God loves us. We know that Christ will never leave us. We know the Spirit is working through us. We know the Lord is coming to get us and take us home with Him. We know the victory will be ours. Let us live like victors! We are more than conquerors through Him who loves us. Now, let us show it to the world.

Renewed Faith

The church needs a renewed faith. Our faith must be renewed on many different levels. To this point in our study we have discussed faith in God, faith in His word, and faith in ourselves. Here again we must restate the issue at hand: (1) God will give the increase. Do we believe this or not? (2) God's word is the power of God unto salvation. Do we believe this or not? (3) The Lord can prepare us and mold us into becoming great soul winners for Jesus. Do we believe this or not?

To each question we probably answered "yes." And I do not doubt the sincerity of the answer. But at some point faith must be put into action. "Faith without works is dead" (James 2:20, 26)

So, if we believe these things to be true, what are we missing?

Renewed Zeal

Zeal, beloved, we need greater zeal! Zeal without knowledge is incomplete (see Romans 10:1-3). So also is knowledge without zeal. One may know the Bible through and through; yet, if he has no zeal to share it, what profit is his knowledge?

I have been in congregations wherein we had some excited Christians, and we had some who were not excited. Some were full of ideas for church growth, and some were full of criticisms to shoot down the ideas. Some were filled with love, while some had left their first love. Some were on fire for the Lord, and some were as cold as ashes.

Here is what I learned: *my* zeal is not dependent upon *their* zeal. I can be as zealous as possible within my personal sphere of influence whether they choose to be zealous or not. Granted, this is a challenge. It is very easy to become discouraged by another's actions.

In order to live this way, I must first take ownership of my attitude. I cannot allow another person to determine the way I feel about the Lord and His mission. I will influence my circle of friends, family, and brethren for good or for evil. I will help them go to heaven, or I will help them go to hell.

Just as I cannot control your attitude, I cannot allow you to control mine. When I have this mindset, I can be as zealous as possible even if others within my home congregation are not as zealous as me. My brethren may not go along with my ideas. They may not appreciate new ideas. But I can still operate under the premise of "each one reach one." I can still seek souls for Christ, even if my ideas for church growth are not accepted. My zeal does not have to change, and my efforts do not have to begin and end with the attitude of others in the local congregation.

Newsflash: not everyone is going to like your ideas. Not everyone is going to be involved in the ideas they do like. When you deal with a plurality of people you are going to have differences of opinions. This is why we must take the focus off of the group – the church – and place it upon the individual – me, myself, and I. Each one, reach one.

I can and must remain optimistic and hopeful about saving souls, even if my brethren seem to be cold and indifferent. Joshua and Caleb did not allow the other ten spies to change their conviction in what God could do. We must not allow another's pessimism to overcome our optimism in the Lord.

We all need encouragement. I know that "iron sharpens iron." God will use us to sharpen others and make sure that others are in our lives to sharpen us.

The point is this: in a congregation wherein zeal seems to be lacking, it has to start somewhere. Let it begin with you. Allow God to use your influence to light a fire in others. But, be patient. Sometimes a fire must start slowly before it begins to blaze – especially if the wood has been dampened!

What if my ideas are not accepted? Who cares! Just keep saving souls. Keep studying and continuing to encourage others and people will take notice of your good work and your influence will only increase. God will use you to revive that congregation. Allow Him to use you!

So many times we can get distracted over things of secondary importance. Matters of lesser importance can cause us to lose heart or become disgruntled. You can handle that easily enough by allowing your heart to be filled with the grace of God. Become a recipient of grace and you will be able to bestow grace. The parable of the unmerciful servant teaches us that those who truly appreciate grace will receive it and bestow it upon others (see Matthew 18:23-35).

Seek to know God truly. We must know God truly, if we wish to show Him to the world and to our brethren. God will use us to affect tremendous change within our sphere of influence. God will use us to change the world one soul at a time.

Remember: the change you hope to affect in others must begin with you. Be the change you hope to see in others.

In Conclusion

What can *you* do to make a difference? If you have replaced faith with pessimism – "repent and believe the gospel!" Be zealous for good works and God will use you to encourage and provoke faith in others.

Paul and his fellow preachers were able to endure everything they suffered and any amount of opposition because they were "Always bearing about in the body the dying of the Lord Jesus, that the life also of Jesus might be made manifest in our body" (2 Corinthians 4:10).

In Paul's weakness he was strong, because the Lord was his source of strength (see 2 Corinthians 12:7-10). He kept the cross within his heart and thus faithfully faced any foe from without.

The devil has filled this world with enough pessimism and doubt. He is seeking to fill your heart with it too. Don't let him. The only way the devil can win is if we let him. Allow God to fill your heart with faith, hope, and love; and be zealous to share it!

"Finally, my brethren, be strong in the Lord, and in the power of his might" (Ephesians 6:10).

Discussion Questions for Chapter Six

1.) Discuss the expectations you have for yourself as a Christian.

2.) Discuss and think upon things you can do to influence your circle of friends, family, and brethren.

3.) How can we prevent our zeal from being dampened by the indifference of others?

4.) How can we remain effective as soul winners even if our ideas are not accepted in our home congregation?

7
The Great Evil of Pessimism

Pessimism is defined as: (1) the belief that the evil in life outweighs the good; (2) the tendency to expect the worst always (Webster's New World Dictionary).

Winston Churchill is credited with saying: "Optimism sees an opportunity in every problem; pessimism sees a problem in every opportunity."

How Has Pessimism Hurt the Church?

➤ **Pessimism is never kept quite.**

When a brother is pessimistic, he will no doubt discourage another brother. Just look at how the ten pessimistic spies let their voices be heard (see Numbers 13-14). Consider the result of their pessimism as well.

As Christians, we are commanded to encourage and provoke one another unto love and good works (Hebrews 10:24). We ask: instead of thinking about all the reasons why a good work *cannot* work, why not consider all the reasons why a good work *can* work?

➤ **Pessimism is a lack of faith in God.**

God is able. God is almighty. Yet, pessimism as an ideology refuses to acknowledge the ability of God.

Pessimists would have us put God in a small box and limit what good He can do. Pessimists will lead us to believe that God is not able to help His church in the works He has instructed us to do. Of course, their agenda is usually to bring about a fundamental change in the teaching and practice of the Lord's church. They believe they have the "better way."

Who is man to question the living God? Who among us dares to question the faithfulness of God? "Yea, let God be found true, but every man a liar" (Romans 2:4).

Pessimists will lead us to believe God has asked something of the church that the church is unable to accomplish. Who are we going to believe? If God believed it impossible to keep His word, He would not have given us His word to keep. If God is not willing to bless the church simply by sowing and watering the seed of the kingdom *today*, He would not have been willing to bless the church *then*. But, seeing that God was willing and did bless the growth of the church in the first century through the preaching of the word, we know that He will also bless us for doing so today.

➢ **Pessimism is a lack of faith in God's wisdom.**

Pessimists do not believe the Bible. Pessimists trust in their own disbelief rather than the word of God. They lean upon their own understanding.

If we are to accomplish anything, it will be because we have trusted God and kept His word. But, trusting in God is not always easy. Sometimes, we may be required to suffer for our faith.

Paul wrote, "For therefore we both labour and suffer reproach, because we trust in the living God, who is the Saviour of all men, specially of those that believe" (1 Timothy 4:10).

Despite the persecution we may suffer, if we are going to be the followers of Christ, we must trust in His Father's plan. We must put our trust in Him. "The Lord is my rock, and my fortress, and my deliverer; my God, my strength, in whom I will trust; my buckler, and the horn of my salvation, and my high tower" (Psalm 18:2)

➤ **Pessimism has led to "liberalism" in the church.**

Liberals seek to change God's plan because their pessimistic ways have them believing His plan cannot work. Liberals change God's plan because they would rather trust their disbelief than the unwavering hand of God.

Ironically, their call-word is "love." One of these days I may write a book with this title, "Loving Liberals: They'll Love You to Death." And I would put a picture of the Grim Reaper on the cover!

Liberals claim to be loving people, and they put on a false persona of love. But, allow a stand to be made against their treachery and their true colors will appear. They simply cannot be happy unless they are getting their way – and their way must be unquestioned.

How does such a person or group take over a congregation? The take-over begins by sowing seeds of doubt and discouragement. They attack anything that resembles the "old paths." They seek to implement a new style of worship and preaching. They seek to eliminate anything not in line with their agenda.

Liberals divide and conquer. They are smart enough to know a house divided cannot stand. Thus, they seek to divide. Instead of trying to reach a soul for Christ, their time is spent trying to convert a brother or sister to their agenda.

Ultimately, they seek to take over the leadership of a congregation. Once that happens, it is simply a matter of time before the entire nature of the congregation is changed in the name of progress.

Does any of this sound familiar? Have you ever experienced something like this? Such experiences began because someone who was pessimistic spoke their doubt and disbelief louder and longer than those who trusted in the Lord. My brethren, "these things ought not to be."

➢ **Pessimism will also lead to "do-nothing-ism."**

One becomes a do-nothing because at some point pessimism has told them: "You are not going to make a difference anyway, so why bother?"

Do-nothings usually stew over all the reasons a good work will fail, rather than to attempt to do the work. Sometimes a do-nothing will let his voice be heard through harsh murmurings and criticisms. Rather than attempt to fix the problem, he would rather *do nothing.*

The Bible teaches us to be "doers of the word and not hearers only" (James 1:21). Do-nothings stop at hearing. In fact, their hearts can be so hardened that they will even close their ears to keep from hearing.

Both liberalism and do-nothing-ism are sinful. In both cases, one has a lack of faith in God and His goodness. In both cases, one has transgressed God's plan and the work of the church is badly maimed and left for dead.

How Has Pessimism Hindered the Spread of the Gospel?

Pessimism has discredited the validity of mission work in the United States. We are told the gospel cannot have the same effect stateside as it does in foreign fields. Yet, every time the gospel is obeyed it has the same effect – whether in the United States or anywhere.

People in this country have souls *too*. We are commanded to go into the entire world; but pessimists tell us the gospel cannot have the effect it once did, and that we must seek other fields. How glad we Christians in America ought to be for those optimists who told us the story of Jesus!

Pessimism has caused many brethren to believe that things can never again be like the "glory days" of the church. We have heard of times when the church was the fastest growing religious body in America. We are told by pessimists that it will never be that way again. However, if we will work with the same degree of faithfulness with which those brethren worked, the same God who blessed them will also bless us.

Pessimism has kept churches from embracing new ideas. We know no benefit in "new doctrines," but new ideas can be extremely beneficial in stimulating growth. Pessimists say, "It'll never work," even without trying. Truly, they have decided to quit trying.

Pessimism has caused a decline in bus ministries and many other good works that were effective in the past. Pessimists tell us those things worked then but will fail today. Are they afraid of a little work? Are they too stingy with the Lord's money to use it in such ways?

If good works will not succeed today, what will? Is this not the day of salvation (2 Corinthians 6:2)? Is this not the day of the Lord and His church? If we allow pessimists to take away our good works, we might as well sell our buildings, burn our Bibles, and convert to atheism!

Allow me to give you another example – gospel meetings. Our gospel meetings used to last for several days, even weeks at a time. The sermons were soul-saving in nature. A gospel meeting used to be the great evangelistic effort of the congregation for that year. For many congregations, nothing has replaced the gospel meeting in the way of an annual evangelistic effort.

Gospel meetings today usually last for four days; and by the time a meeting is really getting started, it is time to finish. The sermons are for the most part evangelistic. However, we have probably heard some that were not. The crowds are usually smaller and mainly consist of Christians. As a result, the day of the great revival and tent meeting is nearly gone. Sadly, we seldom hear of conversions taking place, or souls being restored as a result of these meetings.

It does not have to be this way. A gospel meeting can still be a great evangelistic effort; but we must be optimistic about the work and put our all into making it a success. Failing to plan is planning to fail. If we will plan for these efforts and truly put our all into them, God will bless us.

In Conclusion

How can one overcome this sinful attitude of pessimism?

♦ We must renew and increase our faith in God.

God will reward our labors while we are here on earth and with an eternal reward in heaven (see Mark 10:29-30). If we sow good things, we will reap good things (Galatians 6:7ff). Let us renew and increase our faith in God's wisdom. God's word will not return void.

"So shall my word be that goeth forth out of my mouth: it shall not return unto me void, but it shall accomplish that which I please, and it shall prosper in the thing whereto I sent it" (Isaiah 55:12).

♦ Let us also renew and increase our faith in people.

Let us start by renewing and increasing our faith in ourselves. Everyone can help someone. To overcome pessimism, we may need to increase our faith in what we can do and how we can help.

We also may need to renew and increase our faith in our brethren. Let us determine to appreciate the good that our brother can do and encourage him in those things rather than tear him down for what we perceive to be his weaknesses. Let us build up the body of Christ and believe in the church and the good we can accomplish if we will work together.

♦ Lastly, let us renew and increase our faith in the lost.

We were once lost and *we* obeyed the gospel. If we could become Christians, they can too.

Keep from coming to conclusions about every lost soul because of one or two bad experiences. Not even the great apostle Paul was able to save everyone. However, he did teach us that if we will determine to do all we can do, we will save some (1 Corinthians 9:22).

"For though I be free from all men, yet have I made myself servant unto all, that I might gain the more. And unto the Jews I became as a Jew, that I might gain the Jews; to them that are under the law, as under the law, that I might gain them that are under the law; To them that are without law, as without law, (being not without law to God, but under the law to Christ,) that I might gain them that are without law. To the weak became I as weak, that I might gain the weak: I am made all things to all men, that I might by all means save some. And this I do for the gospel's sake, that I might be par-taker thereof with you" (1 Corinthians 9:19-23).

Discussion Questions for Chapter Seven

1.) What is pessimism?

2.) What harm will pessimism do to the church?

3.) How will pessimism affect the work of the church in preaching the gospel?

4.) How can we prevent pessimism from influencing our attitude and work for Christ?

8

Father Knows Best

To what extent are we willing to trust God? Are we willing to trust His plan for church growth? God's people need to be assured, possibly reassured, of God's wisdom for church growth. Our Father really does know best.

The Right Mission

Our Father gave His church the right mission. The salvation of souls is without doubt the noblest mission, the highest calling, and the gravest responsibility ever known to mortal man.

One's soul is his most precious possession. The Savior once asked:

"For what is a man profited, if he shall gain the whole world, and lose his own soul? or what shall a man give in exchange for his soul?" (Matthew 16:26)

To gain the whole world and all its prized possessions at the expense of losing one's soul would be the greatest tragedy and most suffered loss one could ever incur.

To secure the salvation of the soul, the truth must be taught. Souls are saved by obeying the truth (1 Peter 1:22). Therefore, "receive with meekness the engrafted word, which is able to save your souls" (James 1:21). But, how are lost souls going to hear and receive the gospel without someone to proclaim His word (Romans 10:14)?

God has entrusted this responsibility to His church. The primary work of the church is to make sure precious souls have a chance to hear the saving gospel of Christ. It falls on the church to make sure the lost have the opportunity to obey the gospel. Who shall preach truth if we refuse? Who shall convert the sinner from the error of his way if we choose not to take our mission seriously?

Our Lord did not build a social club, or community recreation center. He built a hospital for sin-sick souls to come and be healed.

The Life-Saving Station

Allow me to speak in a parable – the parable of the life-saving station (the parable does not originate with me, but it is worth sharing).

A treacherous coastline was known for the many crashes which occurred there. Ships seemed to have a most difficult time navigating the rocks along the shore.

Some survivors of these shipwrecks decided a life-saving station needed to be built and that they would staff it in case of future wrecks. The only purpose they had in mind was to save lives. It was to be a life-saving station.

The little station was very successful and did a lot of good for many years. It grew. Others wanted to be a part of the life-saving work.

Some decided that they needed to have some recreational activities to occupy their time and to please their children. Before long, a gymnasium, game room, and tennis court appeared. They then decided to build a golf course. The life-saving station had become a social club – a country club.

Wrecks continued to occur. But no one seemed to care. The members of the life-saving station were now preoccupied by the various obligations of running a country club. The facilities and all the activities became the new purpose of the group.

The old life-saving station which did so much good for so many years was officially a thing of the past. Newer, nicer facilities were built. More people belonged. But no one was ever saved from the rocky shores again.

Have we ceased to be a life-saving station? Have we become more focused upon social and recreational activities than the work of saving souls?

Those of us who work with our youth in various activities and teaching opportunities need to be very careful that we do not lose sight of the mission of the church with all of the various recreational and social activities we provide them. Let us determine not to raise a generation which doesn't know the difference between a life-saving station and a social club.

The Right Method

Our Father knows the best method. *"As you go...,"* the Savior commanded (Matthew 28:19). The church is to grow as we go.

The church grows in souls as Christians go throughout the world, letting their light shine (Matthew 5:16), teaching publicly, and from house to house (Acts 20:20). The church grows stagnant, bitter, and complacent when they stay at home and are consumed by the ways of the world.

Why do churches quarrel? I submit to you that one major reason for such infighting is often because a congregation with its many members never "gets it" as pertaining to their evangelistic responsibilities.

We have become consumed with everything but going into the world and winning a soul for Christ. We spend thousands of dollars and countless hours on everything but evangelism! Have we ceased to be a life-saving station?

The right method involves every member being a go-getter. Both male and female Christians can be soul winners. Aquila and Priscilla were both soul winners.

Both young and old Christians can be soul winners. Timothy and Paul were both soul winners. Young Christians will always need older Christians to help them and set for them the right example as soul winners.

A Christian is never too old to win a soul for Christ! Christians are never too young to be teachers of Christ. In fact, while Christians are young they have a golden opportunity to invite numerous friends from grade school and/or college on almost a daily basis to church services and/or Bible studies.

Lessons Learned from the Parable of the Talents
Matthew 25:14-30

- Every Christian can be placed into one of these three categories, for each of us has been given an opportunity to serve God faithfully throughout life.

- Each person is not given the same measure of opportunity, and yet, each person is expected to be faithful in the measure of opportunity given.

- The Lord will reward His servants who are faithful in the opportunities they are given and will continue to bless them accordingly.

- The Lord knows those who squander their opportunities to serve Him and will punish them accordingly.

- What we do with our opportunities to serve the Lord will determine where we spend our eternity.

We must have a vision to seize the opportunity for a harvest of souls. When Jesus looked upon those precious ones coming to Him from Sychar:

"Say not ye, There are yet four months, and then cometh harvest? behold, I say unto you, Lift up your eyes, and look on the fields; for they are white already to harvest" (John 4:35).

What shall we do with our opportunities? How are we using our religious freedom? How are we using our wealth? How are we using our time? How are we using the blessing of modern technology? We have advantages at our fingertips never before known to the world. What are we doing with these advantages?

The monumental truth we learn from the Parable of the Talents is the accountability each man has to God for the opportunities he has been given. God has provided us with means for taking the gospel into the world in ways which only could have been dreamed about a generation ago. How are we using life's precious moments? What are we doing with our opportunities?

The Right Message

Our Father knows the best message. God chose gospel preaching (1 Corinthians 1:18-21). Go and preach the gospel (Mark 16:15). Preach repentance (Mark 6:12). Preach not yourself (2 Corinthians 4:5). Preach Christ crucified (1 Corinthians 1:23). Preach the church and kingdom He established (Acts 19:8). There remains no more effective, no other prescribed, no other guaranteed, and no other authorized way to bring the lost to Jesus than by preaching unto them the whole counsel of God.

Seeing that we have already devoted a chapter to "Preaching that Saves" we will not spend a lot of time going over the same point again. However, I would like to remind you of the value of preaching and teaching the cross. It is a powerful message. Study the biblical text, sermons, and other good materials. Equip yourself with a thorough knowledge of the cross and share it as often as you can.

The Right Mentality

Our Father exemplifies the best mentality for His church. God gave no boundaries (Acts 1:8). God loves every soul, and every soul has a right to hear the gospel. Heaven will have representatives of every nation, kindred, people and tongue (Revelation 7:9).

For His church to have the right mentality, we must have the attitude that every soul is important to God. The only boundaries which remain are those we have given ourselves.

God has given the church the means for growth in the gospel, the promise of increase if we sow and water, and the confidence to go into the uttermost parts of the world. Why, therefore, would we place a mental boundary by saying the church cannot grow in this place or that place when God has given us the wisdom to grow even in the darkest places on earth?

As God said to Joshua, let Him say unto us, "Have not I commanded thee? Be strong and of a good courage; be not afraid, neither be thou dismayed: for the LORD thy God is with thee whithersoever thou goest" (Joshua 1:9).

The right mentality can exist in a big church or a little church. Big churches need to be careful not to become complacent with their material possessions, and small churches must be careful not to become depressed at their lack of material wealth.

Wealthy churches may come to believe faithfulness in God is unnecessary and poor churches may believe God cannot do anything with their limited resources. In both cases the truth about God is not being considered.

The ministry of Jesus was effective because He knew God. He was like God in character and in purpose. If we hope to be effective in our ministries, we too must reveal the Father to the world. We must know Him and strive to be like Him. Truly, this is the right mentality that will lead to the growth of churches whether they are big or small, rich or poor.

In Conclusion

Our God knows how to save souls. He knows the mission, method, message, and mentality we are to have in order to grow. His plan will work in large congregations and small congregations. We simply need to do our part. If we will dedicate ourselves to saving souls and bringing the lost to Jesus through personal evangelism, the Lord's church will grow.

We do not need 1,000 programs and a "staff" with fifteen ministers to grow. I sometimes wonder if these "staffs" don't lead to a "staff" infection in the local congregation! We do need faith and trust in our Father's wisdom and plan. Let us go to work, brethren!

As we walk in His light, He will ever be with us – even unto the end of the world (Matthew 28:18-20). As we keep His word, God will bless us and keep us!

"For whatsoever is born of God overcometh the world: and this is the victory that overcometh the world, even our faith" (1 John 5:4).

Discussion Questions for Chapter Eight

1.) God is the greatest "church growth expert" of all (T/F).

2.) Discuss the "parable" of the life-saving station. How can we prevent this from happening in our home congregations?

3.) Discuss the Parable of the Talents. What should we learn from it and how should it affect our thinking?

4.) What opportunities have recently been presented to you or your congregation? How did you respond?

9
Launch Out!

Imagine being out upon the sea all night, navigating your ship against the waves and winds, hoping at last to catch something, anything. One hour passes by and then another until finally day breaks, and still you have taken in nothing. By this time, you are tired, discouraged, ready to call it a day, and for good reason. Surely no one can blame you for wanting to go home and rest a while.

You have been a disciple of Jesus for sometime now, and you notice a swelling crowd gathering to hear Him preach while you are cleaning your nets and putting them away for the next time. He enters into your ship and tells you to pull out a little way from the shore. From there He continues His lesson. You are ready to sit and listen. Maybe later you can go home, clean up, and go to bed. But Jesus asks of you, "Launch out into the deep and let down your nets for a catch" (Luke 5:4). What would you say? Would you obey? Would you enjoy the blessing?

Now, imagine you are a Christian who has been laboring for many years at a congregation, sowing, and watering without seeing much increase for your labors. What do you do? Is now the time to rest from your labors? Would anyone blame you for being discouraged and ceasing from the work?

The disciples at the lake of Gennesaret had two commands to obey in order to receive the one promise that was given.

➢ They had to launch out into the deep.

➢ They had to let down their nets to receive a catch.

The discouraged Christian still has only two commands to obey for the promise to be granted (Mar 16:15-16).

➢ He must go into the world.

➢ He must preach the gospel.

Peter's reply at Gennesaret was probably not very different from the reply we would get from a discouraged Christian. You can imagine such a one saying, "But I've worked all this time and seen no response." These two scenarios are very much alike.

The Discouraged Christian May Need to Change

In both instances, there was a need for change. *Not all change is sinful.* The disciples needed a change *of attitude* (Luke 5:5). Discouraged and possibly tired, they saw no need to try again.

The disciples needed a change in attitude that would produce a change *in action.* They were on the shore washing their nets and their ships were standing idle. No fisherman will catch any fish this way. They needed to launch out and let down their nets.

A Christian or congregation may need to make similar changes in order to grow. If we are discouraged, tired, and sitting idly, we need to make a change. Our thoughts, attitudes, and actions need changing. We must know assuredly that we will not save a single soul if we are sitting at home discouraged and disgusted.

The Discouraged Christian May Need an Increased Faith

The discouraged brother needs reminding of the value of an "at thy word" type of faith. Maybe he has toiled all the night and taken nothing. Maybe he is in need of much wanted rest from these labors.

It is discouraging to face the grim reality that your home congregation is dying. One wonders "why" and some assign blame. When, in reality, we simply need to keep launching out, for our Lord has promised a catch. The blessing remains, "Sow and water, and God will give the increase."

The disciples had to believe Christ would bless them. So too must we believe that He will bless our efforts. The same Jesus that gave that great catch of fish will provide His church with a great harvest of souls if we will "go and preach."

The Discouraged Christian May Need to Become More Obedient

The disciples and discouraged brethren share in their need for obedience. Faith apart from obedience is not really faith. True faith is obedient faith.

Even though Jesus issued the command, the disciples still had to launch out into the deep. They had freewill to choose to obey or not to obey.

Christ commanded, instructed, and promised. It was up to the disciples to believe, obey, and receive.

Let us look at this very simply. Christ commanded them to go to the place where they would find the fish. Once there, the disciples had to let down their nets.

Any fisherman knows that he must go to the water in order to catch any fish. Likewise, we must keep going into the world if we are to save the lost. Christ has commanded us to go to the lost and they are in the world. We must go to the place where we are going to find the lost. Just as the fishermen had to go into the deep to find the fish, we must go into the world to find the lost.

Once there, Christians are to preach the gospel (Mark 16:15). Just as the fishermen could not catch any fish without their nets being in the water, the sinner cannot be saved without the gospel being preached (Romans 1:16). The gospel is our net. We must go to the deep and let down our net.

The fishermen did this and received the promised catch. In fact, the catch that they received far exceeded their expectations. The only thing left to do was to praise the Lord.

If we will do as He has said, the church will also receive her promised reward. We too will be found praising the Lord for doing far above anything we could have imagined (see Ephesians 3:20-21).

The Discouraged Christian Must Remain Ready at All Times

One last common thought to notice is the need to be ready. The four disciples were ready. They had the ships, the nets, and plenty of help.

Churches must be ready to grow. Christians must be ready to see results. We already have the means of going, the gospel of Christ to preach, and the promise of increase from the Father. Perhaps what we lack is a ready spirit to do the will of God (2 Corinthians 8:11) and to give an answer for our faith (1 Peter 3:15).

We must also have fellow helpers (see 2 Corinthians 1:24; 3 John 8). These disciples had plenty of help. A congregation also needs every member helping and active in the cause of Christ. Let us be laborers together with God (1 Corinthians 3:9).

Would it not be reasonable to say that many Christians are afraid to teach lost souls because they fear they do not know enough to teach? For some, this could be a true and legitimate fear. For others, it could be that they simply do not know how to teach.

One helpful suggestion is to teach what you know. Instead of worrying over everything you do not know or are uncomfortable to say with certainty, why not stick to teaching those things you can say with certainty? Be ready to teach what you know. As you grow, you will become more prepared and you will be able to teach even more.

In Conclusion

What was the result of the disciples' change, faith, obedience, and readiness? A great catch was enjoyed (Luke 5:6). They ceased doubting, believed even more in Jesus, gave Him all the glory, and forsook all to follow Him (vv.7-11).

What will be the result for us if we make necessary changes, have an "at thy word" type of faith, obey the commission of our Savior, and are ready for the work? Souls will be saved. Sinful attitudes, murmurings, and doubts will give way to a new day of confident assurance in God's word and His willingness to use us. The church will grow, and our joy will only increase in the day of Christ when we are reunited with those we helped bring to the Lord (see 2 Corinthians 1:14; Philippians 2:16).

At our Lord's word, may we launch out in love and tell the world about a Savior who died and lives again!

"I am with you alway, even unto the end of the world. Amen" (Matthew 28:20).

Discussion Questions for Chapter Nine

1.) What two things were required of the fisherman in order to receive the catch? What two things are required of the church in order to save souls?

2.) What might a discouraged Christian need to change in order to become more effective?

3.) Discuss Ephesians 3:20-21 in the context of this narrative from the life of Christ.

4.) What are some things we can do to be ready to go into the world and preach/teach the gospel?

10
Excited, Encouraged, and Effective

(A Study of the Church of Christ at Jerusalem)

In recent years, we have probably had the opportunity to witness some congregations grow in attendance, even while teaching unsound doctrine and acting unfaithfully. Weaker brethren will see this increase and push for their home congregations to do likewise.

Each congregation has the option of forsaking God's plan for growth, turning a blind eye to sin, turning to entertainment, gimmicks or other "gospels" and seeing an increase in their attendance. Each congregation is an independent, self-governing body of believers.

In spite of this trend, our conviction remains to grow by doing right. The church of Christ at Jerusalem in the first century A.D. stands out as an exemplary congregation that grew by following God's plan. This is perhaps the finest congregation of the Lord's church ever to exist. It was the first. And these brethren had to overcome much in order to grow, yet they remained excited, encouraged, and effective.

What did this congregation do in order to grow? Did they permit false teachers? Did they submit to the whimsies of the religious consumer? Did they bow to the pressure of the world and worldly-minded brethren? No! A thousand times, No!

They Grew by Hearing and Obeying Gospel Preaching

On Pentecost, in Jerusalem, Peter unveiled the gospel: "Then they that gladly received his word were baptized: and the same day there were added unto them about three thousand souls" (Acts 2:41).

They not only heard and obeyed the gospel, but continued steadfastly in the apostles' doctrine and fellowship (Acts 2:42). "And the Lord added to the church daily such as should be saved" (Acts 2:47).

The church continued preaching the word in season and out of season. Peter and John continued preaching the gospel of Christ in Jerusalem despite the risks of being thrown into prison (Acts 3:1-4:3).

"Howbeit many of them which heard the word believed; and the number of the men was about ("came to be" NKJV) five thousand" (Acts 4:4).

Thus, the church of Christ grew to be 5,000 in just a short amount of time. How did they do it? They preached the word and continued steadfastly in the word. But let us not discount the mighty hand of God as He revealed Himself through these people. We too must allow God to reveal Himself through us.

They Grew by Being United in the Cause of Christ

The church began with one accord and remained in one accord (Acts 4:5-5:11). Such unity provided the necessary environment for increased opportunities and church growth.

"And by the hands of the apostles were many signs and wonders wrought among the people; (and they were all with one accord in Solomon's porch...And believers were the more added to the Lord, multitudes both of men and women)" (Acts 5:12-14).

For the Jerusalem congregation, the idea of fellowship truly defined their relationship with each other. Fellowship was the bond that kept them united and active in the cause of Christ.

On one occasion, when this fellowship could have been threatened by the egos of Ananias and Saphira (Acts 5:1-11), the Lord corrected them through Peter, swiftly and decisively, reminiscent of the days of Israel in the wilderness. This ought to prove to us how important our unity is to the Lord.

They Grew by Being Evangelistic

The church filled Jerusalem with the doctrine of Christ (Acts 5:28). "And daily in the temple, and in every house, they ceased not to teach and preach Jesus Christ" (Acts 5:42).

Did you catch that? They went to the temple, where the religious people were and taught them; and they went from house to house. They did not cease to teach and preach Jesus.

They did not lose sight of their mission. Our brethren did not cease or slow down in the proclamation of the gospel and, therefore, "in those days the number of the disciples was multiplied" (Acts 6:1).

We must observe that the Lord's church in Jerusalem was not carried away with programs to get people involved. Every member appears to have had a desire to share their salvation with others.

It is probably safe to say that the Lord's church in Jerusalem was as evangelistic as any congregation has ever been. They had an "every day in every home" mentality to evangelism. Is it any wonder that they grew from 130 souls to 5,000 in such a short amount of time?

We can do the same today. But, each member must have a desire to share their salvation within their sphere of influence. If we will only do this, brethren, we will grow.

They Grew by Overcoming Internal Conflict

That they did not lose sight of their mission is made clear in the way they handled a dispute which arose concerning the care of the Grecian widows. The apostles would not leave the ministry of the word to serve tables. This dispute was resolved quickly and everyone was pleased (Acts 6:5).

From this conflict and subsequent resolution, we learn how it is possible for everyone to be pleased at the same time from the same decision.

◆ Everyone was pleased because each person wanted the conflict settled.

◆ Everyone was pleased because the matter was handled quickly by godly men.

◆ Everyone was pleased because it did not cause a division.

◆ Everyone was pleased because the work of saving souls did not cease.

106

"And the word of God increased; and the number of the disciples multiplied in Jerusalem greatly; and a great company of the priests were obedient to the faith" (Acts 6:7).

A second instance of overcoming internal conflict was the matter that arose over Gentile circumcision (Acts 15). Again a strong leadership took action (Acts 15:6); the gospel was upheld (Acts 15:7-20); and a decision was reached that pleased everyone (Acts 15:22).

The matter was dealt with quickly, decisively, and by the word of God. Such a response to internal conflict should always be pleasing to a church determined to do the will of God.

The dispute over Gentile converts and circumcision not only gives us an example of a church being in one accord (Acts 15:25) and reaching a decision from God's word, it also teaches us how God is pleased with such reasoning and resulting decisions (see Acts 15:28).

Sometimes we are tried by internal conflict which is more devilish in nature. In his book *Antagonists in the Church*, Kenneth C. Haugk writes:

"Antagonists are individuals who, on the basis of nonsubstantive evidence, go out of their way to make insatiable demands, usually attacking the person or performance of others. These attacks are selfish in nature, tearing down rather than building up, and are frequently directed against those in a leadership capacity."

Antagonists will attempt to bully the preacher, leadership, and the congregation. When confronted by such a bully, we must take strength in the Lord and stand together in honor and in preserving the dignity of His bride.

To manage church conflict properly we must prepare ourselves spiritually and mentally. We must have our minds focused and our attitudes must be godly, so we can give our attention to the conflict at hand and handle it biblically.

Spiritually-minded people will be better able to identify the parties and problems at play and evaluate the best approach to take.

If these examples from Acts teach us anything, they teach us to be assertive. Be assertive with "self" first and then be assertive in managing the conflict.

When resolving the conflict, be a good listener. As in Acts 6, seek to understand the issues that are responsible for the conflict. Keep in mind what you hope to accomplish, and resolve the matter in a way that will bring people closer to God and the church into a greater state of peace with themselves.

They Grew by Overcoming External Conflict

The church in Jerusalem continued to grow even though they had been persecuted by the rulers of the Jews and more severely by men like Saul of Tarsus. They had witnessed many brethren scatter from Jerusalem. Yet, the persecution they suffered not only hastened the preaching of the gospel in other places, it also strengthened the resolve of the Lord's church in Jerusalem.

Amid persecution, the Jerusalem congregation *rested* in their relationship and was *comforted* by their faith in the Lord. Observe:

"Then had the churches rest throughout all Judaea and Galilee and Samaria, and were edified; and walking in the fear of the Lord, and in the comfort of the Holy Ghost, were multiplied" (Acts 9:31).

Concerning the reality of conflict with the world, let's face it, we will be forced to decide between God and society. If you love the truth and teach the truth, you will be hated by those who hate the truth.

Jesus has told us He did not come "to send peace, but a sword." Truth will be controversial because the world does not love or receive it. The world hated Jesus; and He has told us that it will hate us as well.

With this being said and understood, we must prepare ourselves and brace ourselves for conflict with the world. All who would live godly in Christ will suffer persecution (2 Timothy 3:12). It comes with the territory. Let us embrace it and face it with courage from above.

The church in Jerusalem decided to handle the hatred they faced with steadfastness and a view to the coming reward; and the church grew because of this. We cannot do anything about the way others will treat us or respond to us. We have no control over that. But, we do have control over the way we handle ourselves in such situations and whether or not we will remain focused on our mission and our goal of heaven. Let us work to control what we can, and pray for God to control the things we cannot.

They Grew by Never Giving Up

After Paul had been on three missionary journeys, he returned to Jerusalem and was informed of how the church in that great city was continuing to grow. The elders declared, "Thou seest, brother, how many thousands of Jews there are which believe…" (Acts 21:20)

The declaration made by the elders proves how this congregation kept growing. They continued to grow even while having to overcome hardships which many of today's Christians in America could only imagine.

The devil would have loved nothing more than for this church to give up. He would love nothing more than to see churches today give up.

There are three things the devil is trying to do:

➢ The devil is trying to keep souls from becoming Christians.

➢ The devil is trying to entice Christians to return to the world.

➢ If the devil cannot keep us out of the church, or get us to leave the church, he will be perfectly happy to cause us to become indifferent and useless in the church.

We must never become indifferent to what we are doing. We must never give up on our work or our goal. As long as there is breath in our bodies, and mental soundness, there is an opportunity to do good works unto all men (Galatians 6:10).

In Conclusion

The Jerusalem church in the first century is an excellent example of how a church will grow by doing right. They did not need to turn a blind eye to sin; they needed no gimmicks; they did not need to entertain the children of Jerusalem; they needed no alterations to the gospel to make it more palatable to the worldly-minded religious consumer.

Our brethren were steadfast and resolved in the gospel message and blessed by the goodness of God because of it. God added to the church daily because the word was being taught and obeyed daily. The Jerusalem church understood that evangelism was an everyday responsibility and each member took responsibility to do the work.

The Lord's church at Jerusalem provides a great source of encouragement and inspiration for Christians everywhere. No matter what was thrown at them, they just kept on going. No matter what, they remained excited, encouraged, and effective.

"For I am not ashamed of the gospel of Christ: for it is the power of God unto salvation to every one that believeth; to the Jew first, and also to the Greek. For therein is the righteousness of God revealed from faith to faith: as it is written, The just shall live by faith" (Romans 1:16-17).

111

Discussion Questions for Chapter Ten

1.) What about the congregation at Jerusalem is outstanding to you?

2.) Is it possible for a congregation to grow today as they did then?

3.) What are some of the things the Jerusalem congregation did that your congregation can do today to bring church growth?

4.) What are some of the things the church in Jerusalem did not do that we see others doing today in the name of church growth?

11
Keeping Worship Spiritual and True

Can we turn to performances and drama in the interest of church growth and please God? Is the method of our worship service meaningless as long as the mood of the worship is meaningful? Does it matter how we worship God?

One area in which we are seeing deviations from biblical truth is in our worship services. Worshipping God in spirit and truth has become secondary to our need to entertain the religious consumer. If performances are permissible in the name of church growth, why is there not the first line of scripture which authorizes a performance as an act of New Testament worship? Once again we must state that such deviations are completely unnecessary for true church growth. As we have learned, the Jerusalem church did not grow because of the song leader or the preacher, but because the congregation took it upon themselves to reach the lost.

If our worship is going to bring forth true spiritual growth it must be directed to God rather than merely an exercise aimed at meeting the supposed felt-needs of the congregant.

In this portion of our study we will give diligence to the manner of worship our Father is seeking. Our worship should be found meaningful in its method and mood as we shall present the importance of both.

Jesus at Jacob's Well

Our study begins near the somewhat obscure Samaritan village of Sychar. Jesus had been to Jerusalem for the first Passover of His earthly ministry (John 2:13). He cleansed the temple of money changers for the first time (vv.14-17), performed miracles (v.23), taught Nicodemus (3:1-21), and tarried for a while in Judea baptizing with His disciples (v.22) – although He did not personally baptize anyone (4:2).

When the time came for Jesus to return north into Galilee to begin His Galilean ministry, He decided to go through Samaria (4:4). About noon, Jesus came upon the outskirts of this village and being wearied from His travel, He stopped to rest near a well of water. It was known as "Jacob's well" (v.6).

A Samaritan woman approached the well and Christ asked her to draw some water for Him. She was startled that a male Jew would ask something of a Samaritan woman and questioned such an action – "For Jews have no dealings with the Samaritans" (John 4:9). Jesus was opportunistic and began to teach this lady of the water of life (vv.10-14), her sinful relationship with a man who was not her husband (vv.15-18), the Father's desire for true worship (vv.19-24), and of His being the Messiah (vv.25-26).

Concerning worship, evidently this woman had given thought to the subject for sometime. Perceiving Jesus to be a prophet, she took the opportunity to raise a question as to the proper place of worship (John 4:20).

She had been taught that Mt. Gerizim was as good a place to worship as Jerusalem. She was wrong. Jesus said, "You worship what you do not know" (v.22).

Today many precious souls worship or perform for one another due to a lack of biblical knowledge and understanding. As Christians, we cannot justify or condone this error. Christ did not seek to justify or condone the Samaritans worship at Gerizim. Rather, He sought to teach her about true worship and said it would consist of both spirit and truth.

All who are willing to study can understand Christ's teachings and that only true worship – conducted in spirit and truth – is pleasing to God. God is pleased with only one specific formula for worship – spirit and truth.

What Does It Mean to Worship in Spirit?

Worship is induced by emotions of the human heart. These emotions are to be channeled properly, decently, and in order (1 Corinthians 14:40). We must learn the difference between worshiping with emotion and emotionalism.

Emotionalism does nothing more than appeal to human emotions. Worship is more than emotionalism. Worship is metaphorically defined as "a bowing of the knees to God" (cf. Ephesians 3:14; Revelation 4:20; Revelation 5:14). Worship is "homage rendered to God and the ascended Christ."

Worship should be devoted to honoring God, not solely appealing to personal emotions. When "worship" becomes a performance it ceases to be worship and becomes a performance. In fact, worship, if properly conducted, should appeal more to human reasoning than emotion. Sadly, it has become a common practice among many congregations to disregard the need for reasoning and the role of the thinking mind in worship. God does not want us ignorant of His will.

Using our minds to think about our worship while we worship does not negate emotion in our worship. To the contrary, it merely limits the emotions we use.

No doubt we are to worship with the right emotion and attitude – love, sincerity, humility, reverence, and thanksgiving. When we worship with the right emotion, we will have the right effect on the emotions of those assembled with us.

However, an atmosphere conducive to worship is not the primary aim of true worship. True worship is not for the purpose or hope of arousing some type of emotion in those present. Any action done for the purpose of stimulating another's emotions, rather than being devoted to the honor and glory of God, is not an act of true worship.

We should worship with the right emotion because we love God and are thankful for the spiritual blessings we enjoy in Christ. Joy will be evident. People will be glad to be there. Souls will be saved in such assemblies. Hearts will be pricked. Surely nothing is wrong with such results.

Worship can be meaningful in its mood and still be conducted in the truth and spirit God is seeking. As Jesus taught this Samaritan lady, the location of the worship is not what is important in Christian worship, but the location of the heart. If our heart is in the right place, we will have the proper emotion.

What Does It Mean to Worship in Truth?

What is truth? Christ said truth is God's word: "Sanctify them by Your truth. Your word is truth" (John 17:17).

God's word has been revealed in various covenants of vast differences. Which portion of God's word must be our authority for worship? Are we to worship as they did in the days of the patriarchs? Are Christians to worship according to God's word given to the Jews at Sinai? Or, is New Testament worship exclusively New Testament?

The truth spoken of by Jesus at Sychar was a truth soon coming. As Christ was speaking, Jews were still bound by the covenant God gave at Sinai. Therefore, the covenant God made with Israel could not have been the worship Christ had in mind. This truth was to come by Jesus, as "the law was given through Moses, but grace and truth came through Jesus Christ" (John 1:17).

This does not mean Moses did not speak truth, but the truth which Moses prophesied (Deuteronomy 18:15-18) would become fulfilled in Christ. Moses was the mediator of "the shadow of good things to come, but the body is of Christ" (Colossians 2:17).

Man cannot worship according to the shadow any more than he can eat and be filled from the shadow of a ham hanging in a grocery store. To worship in truth is to worship according to the substance, not the shadow. The old law has been forever placed in the shadow of the cross (Hebrews 8:13). Truth is in Jesus (Ephesians 4:21). We are to follow Paul as he followed Christ (1 Corinthians 11:1), not as he

117

followed Abraham, Moses, or David. To worship in truth is to worship in Christ according to His word and as determined by His covenant.

Man cannot worship today according to any other covenant. All other covenants have died and we are free to be married to Christ (Romans 7:1-6). No man is authorized to bind a commandment, use an example, or make an inference for worship outside of the covenant we have with Christ.

No man is authorized to usurp the authority Christ has over His bride (Ephesians 5:23). To say man must keep the Sabbath, tithe, or worship with a mechanical instrument of music because it was authorized through the old law is to make the authority found in that law of greater force than the law given by Christ. You will recall how on the Mount of Transfiguration, in the presence of Moses and Elijah, the Father said of the Son "Here ye Him." Yet, to do such things because Moses wrote them in the law is to listen to Moses rather than Christ.

True worship not only demands the right spirit, but also the right covenant. Man must worship according to the covenant God made with every nation (Matthew 28:18). The new covenant was spoken of by the prophet as being in the future (Jeremiah 31:31-34) and by the writer of Hebrews as being in effect (Hebrews 8:6 ff.; 10:8 ff.). It came into being with Christ's death on the cross as the law was nailed to the cross (Colossians 2:14) and the Testator died (Hebrews 9:15-16).

According to this covenant, we have a Lord's Day (Revelation 1:10). The Lord's Day is the day of His resurrection – the first day of each week (Acts 20:7; 1 Corinthians 16:1-2).

It is not to be forsaken (Hebrews 10:25). On this day, we are commanded to assemble together into one place to worship (1 Corinthians 11:20).

As the first covenant had ordinances of worship, so also does the new covenant. During this solemn assembly, we are authorized through approved examples, direct statements, and proper inference to do certain acts of worship.

We are commanded to pray, sing spiritual songs, give of our material wealth, partake of the Lord's Supper, preach and hear the gospel. We can see that each act is to be independent of the others by the use of the conjunction "*and*." We pray *and* sing (Acts 16:25; 1 Corinthians 14:15; James 5:13). There is to be a breaking of the bread *and* prayers (Acts 2:42). The night the Lord's Supper was instituted they communed (Matthew 26:26-27) *and* sang a hymn (Matthew 26:30).

Each Act in Spirit and Truth

Notice how these acts of worship are divinely given as well as the spirit in which each act is to be followed. We are to pray to our Father (Luke 11:2 ff.) in Christ's name (Ephesians 5:20), thus glorifying the Father (John 14:13). This is the true method for this act of worship. We are to do so with thanksgiving (Ephesians 5:20) and understanding (1 Corinthians 14:15), while remembering one another (James 5:16). These are ways in which this act of worship is done in the true spirit of worship.

Such is the case with our singing. Not only are we commanded to sing, we are told what to sing and how to sing:

119

"Speaking to one another in psalms and hymns and spiritual songs, singing and making melody in your heart to the Lord" (Ephesians 5:19).

Only when we sing the right songs, teaching and admonishing one another with the instrument of the human heart, do we worship with a true method. Only when we make melody in our hearts unto the Lord and with understanding (1 Corinthians 14:15) do we worship in a true spirit.

Also, we should emphasize that every Christian is commanded to sing. Realizing this will keep us from solos, choruses, and praise teams. We are not commanded to assemble for the purpose of being entertained by another's ability. We are each commanded to assemble for the purpose of offering our worship to God – together – in spirit and in truth.

True worship is commanded in our giving. We are to give as we have prospered on the first day of the week (1 Corinthians 16:2). This is according to proper method. We are also to give cheerfully (2 Corinthians 9:7). This is the right emotion. When we give in this way, we worship in spirit and in truth.

We are to examine ourselves as we partake of the Lord's Supper (1 Corinthians 11:28). This self-examination requires the right spirit. We are to do so upon the first day of the week (Acts 20:7) as we are assembled together into one place (1 Corinthians 11:20, 33).

Two emblems are commanded. Both emblems are unleavened – the bread and the fruit of the vine – as there was no leaven in the house at the Passover when the Supper was instituted. Therefore, if we are to follow Christ's example there will be no leaven in the Supper as we partake (cf. Exodus 12:20; Leviticus 23:6; Deuteronomy 16:1-8). We are to do this in remembrance of Him. This again requires the right spirit.

Concerning the act of proclaiming truth, as in any act of worship, the woman cannot usurp the authority given by God to the man. It is not permitted for her to preach in the assembly of the saints (1 Corinthians 14:34-35; 1 Timothy 2:11-12). God has forever established the role of women in the church. We say this not to be deemed chauvinistic, but biblical.

Those who preach are to "speak the truth in love" (Ephesians 4:15). In this inspired text, we see the act of preaching being done with the right spirit – love. We are to speak the truth to His glory (1 Peter 4:11). If truth is not preached, God is not glorified and the worship is not true. If truth is not preached in love, God is not glorified and the worship is not true.

We must not only speak the truth, we must speak the truth in love. Preachers must make known His plan of salvation if they are to be worshiping in spirit and truth.

Hearers are to receive God's truth in a spirit of meekness (James 1:21). When the truth is spoken in love and received in meekness, we can know assuredly God is well pleased with this aspect of our worship.

We live in a time that perhaps more than ever needs a return to sound and doctrinal preaching. The great preacher, J.D. Tant (1861-1941) said many years ago, "Brethren, we are drifting." Brethren, we have drifted! The only recourse is the return of doctrinal preaching.

Worship Is Not a Performance

Understanding that church growth occurs when lost souls are forgiven and added to the church by God, we ask: what does it profit to turn a worship service into a performance?

The ends do not justify the means, for the ends – the salvation of lost souls – cannot be accomplished without the gospel being heard and obeyed. To have a contemporary worship service to boost attendance accomplishes nothing as far as church growth is concerned.

Church growth requires more than a boost in attendance. Moreover, someone who will attend a church service only if they can attend a contemporary service is someone who is attending for the wrong reason.

God must be honored in our worship. When man is honored above God through traditions, doctrines, and commandments of men, the worship becomes "vain" (Matthew 15:9) and an act of "will worship" (Colossians 2:22-23).

God has stipulated the pattern for New Testament worship. Our dedication must be to true worship rather than gimmickry and performances which are encouraged through manmade traditions.

If we compromise on this point to satisfy the religious consumer, inevitably we will find ourselves compromising again on other matters. Such compromises have already placed many on an out of control rollercoaster destined to crash and burn.

On the other hand, if we will truly worship and faithfully teach as we follow Jesus, we have His promise that we will be blessed and we will grow. Let us put our trust in His promises rather than foolish schemes.

In Conclusion

God is seeking true worship and we must determine to worship in spirit and truth. Let us resolve to worship Him with the right emotion, motivation, and guide. Let us worship God as He is seeking and not as we are seeking.

Concerning the holy worship of almighty God, may we have conviction rather than compromise! May the Lord's people worship Him in spirit and truth both now and forevermore!

"I will declare thy name unto my brethren, in the midst of the church will I sing praise unto thee" (Hebrews 2:12).

Discussion Questions for Chapter Eleven

1.) Define *worship*.

2.) Define *performance*.

3.) Discuss the differences in these two differing actions.

4.) Which action – *worship* or *performance* – was Christ concerned with teaching at Sychar?

5.) Are deviations from New Testament worship necessary for the church to grow? What is necessary for church growth?

12
Basic Needs for Church Growth

Each Christian should seek to increase their basic knowledge of things essential for true church growth. We should be thinking of ways to help our home congregation and ways we can secure for a bright future for the Lord's church.

By selecting ten topics to be discussed briefly, and in no certain order, we hope to stimulate thought and increase knowledge among God's children on the subject of church growth.

Biblical Balance

The first point we wish to discuss is *biblical balance*. The idea of balance is often subjective to the one speaking his or her view of a certain subject. Sometimes the idea of balance is used to justify compromises people have made; and anyone who objects to their compromise is unbalanced.

In our case, we regard balance as being the six inch mark on a twelve inch ruler. To be balanced is to remain on the six inch mark. We do not want to go to the left or right of that six inch mark. We might also think about a person walking a tight right. If that person wavers too far to the right or the left he will fall.

We might also use the analogy of a football team. For the team to win, they need to be good at offense, defense, and special teams. They also need to have some good coaches. When everyone works according to their ability, such a team will be hard to beat.

A Balanced Leadership

Elderships must be balanced. A church cannot grow with a minority rule in the eldership. Minority rule will only lead to factions and hard feelings. A house divided cannot stand.

Neither can a church grow if there is an unbiblical majority rule in the eldership. Elderships are not to be democratic, but faithful to the word of God. They must neither be radical or liberal – only faithful. They must be found:

"…holding fast the faithful word as they have been taught, that they may be able by sound doctrine both to exhort and to convince the gainsayers" (Titus 1:9).

God gave us instructions so that *only* such men would serve in this holy capacity (1 Timothy 3:1-7; Titus 1:6-9). Without such men so serving, a congregation will lack the necessary vision and guidance to be productive in the work of the Lord.

Members must remain loyal to their elders as they prove their faithfulness to the Scriptures. According to Paul, we must, "Let the elders that rule well be counted worthy of double honour, especially they who labour in the word and doctrine" (1 Timothy 5:17). But, "Them that sin rebuke before all, that others also may fear" (1 Timothy 5:20). Christians are never commanded by God to yield to an unholy and unfaithful eldership.

Sadly, many times Christians use the sins of an eldership to disguise and cover-up their own sins and their own compromises to the word of God. This "blame game" enables them, they suppose, to go along with unbiblical compromises without appearing to be guilty of any compromise personally. However, this is only a feebleminded attempt to hide personal guilt. Why blame the elders for the sins of the congregation and remain satisfied to say and do nothing to stop the digression? Brethren who play this blame game are not really fooling anyone – especially God. "Be sure your sin will find you out" (Numbers 32:23).

As faithful elderships are selected by faithful congregations, unfaithful elders are selected by unfaithful congregations. The apple does not fall far from the tree. Elderships are the product of the congregation which has selected them "from among them."

A dangerous cycle can occur in congregations which have made unscriptural compromises. If the congregation has become accustomed to an unscriptural practice or doctrine, usually whomever they select from among themselves will also be prone to the same error.

Of course, this is why God has provided the qualifications for elders. He has given us His wisdom in order to keep us from falling into this vicious cycle.

Concerning church growth, a congregation cannot outgrow its leadership. If church growth is important to the elders and if they are very evangelistic, the congregation will follow their example. The elders are truly the shepherds of the sheep. We will follow our shepherds.

Sadly, many an eldership will function as a board of directors and as administrators rather than being shepherds to the people. Their concern is primarily the building and the budget. Usually the only people this type of eldership will oversee are those employed by the church. Brethren, "these things ought not to be."

When an eldership becomes a board of directors instead of functioning as shepherds, their work and influence is undone. To compensate for what they are not doing, elders will begin forming evangelism committees and visitation programs. A deacon or minister or one of the elders will report back to the others accordingly.

Do not misunderstand me. I am not making a blanket statement that any such program or group is sinful or unscriptural. Many of these groups are justifiable and doing a great work; but my point is this: nothing can replace the influence a godly eldership can have upon a congregation as they lead them in the work of the Lord.

The problem as I see it is that it can become very easy for elders to be disconnected from the congregation and from the work of the church. Rather than seeking the straying sheep and making sure the church is being fed the milk and meat of the word personally, the work is given to committees; while things of a secondary nature become of utmost importance to the elders.

While we understand that the elders have a responsibility for taking care of the budget and building, our point is that these things should not take priority over the souls of the flock. Quite frankly, much of the work being done by elders could be done by deacons, or anyone for that matter. Elders must never forget that God has called them to feed the flock and oversee His sheep; not buildings and budgets. Knowing this to be true, godly elders must never lose sight of *why* we have elders in the first place.

Moreover, we tend to practice what we preach against. We preach against the pastoral system of church government, and then we hire a preacher to serve as the pastor. While the elders serve as administrators, the preacher is the one who is shepherding the flock in spiritual matters. While elders meet to discuss the budget, the preacher is seeking the one who has strayed from "the ninety and nine."

While a preacher can and should do the work of an evangelist, much more and greater good can be done if the elders and the preacher are working together by doing their respective roles faithfully.

A Balanced Minister

As faithful elderships will seek faithful preachers, unfaithful elders will seek to hire unfaithful preachers. As the eldership goes, so goes the balance of the congregation. This brings us to preachers. Seeing that we have already devoted a chapter to biblical preaching, let us observe only a couple of points.

Our preachers must be balanced. A preacher determined to turn to the left of God's word will ruin a church and discourage any hope for true growth. Liberalism leads to digression. To digress is to make worse. Obviously, a church is not becoming better if it is being made worse by a liberal and digressive preacher.

Likewise, a preacher determined to turn to the right of God's word will ruin a congregation. Radicalism is a digression from God's word, only in a different direction. The church needs faithful men to stand upon God's word (2 Timothy 2:2).

Paul was such a man, as he said of himself: "Wherefore I take you to record this day, that I am pure from the blood of all men. For I have not shunned to declare unto you all the counsel of God" (Acts 20:26-27).

Our preachers must be free from the blood of all men. They must be found declaring the whole counsel of God. Anything less should be deemed unacceptable.

Balanced in Work

Our works must also be balanced. The Scriptures are profitable "unto every good work" (2 Timothy 3:17), which tells us that there is more than one good work (cf. Ephesians 2:10; Titus 3:8; James 2:18). Therefore, a Christian and a congregation must prove their faith through various good works, with each work moving toward the goal of evangelizing the lost.

The benefit of such a work ethic will lead to well-balanced works and something for everyone to do. When all our eggs are in one basket, it only takes a couple of people to tend to that basket. The more baskets a congregation has, will lead to more jobs being available for other Christians to work. With more jobs available, more people are able to work and fewer people are able to become stagnant, bitter, and complacent.

Have a Positive Atmosphere in the Worship Assembly

Our worship assemblies should never appear cold, inconsiderate, or gloomy. Who among us wants to attend a wake three or four times a week? If our assemblies are full of frowning, unpleasant people, no one will want to attend them either. Such times of worship and fellowship should be overflowing with warmth, friendliness, and an inviting mood.

We must worship with the right emotions at the proper times. Our assemblies should be periods for true and spiritual worship (John 4:23-24), encouragement, righteous provocation unto one another (Hebrews 10:24-25), and consideration for the holiness of our faith (1 Corinthians 14:15).

When we come together into one place to worship God, it is a very holy and special time. Such occasions should manifest our love and appreciation for the Lord, His church, and any visitors and/or children who may be attending. If our worship is derived from a pure heart, our assemblies will be pleasing to God and display such necessary warmth by and to those present.

Have you ever visited a congregation only to have one or two or no one speak to you? I do not know why it is so hard for some us to make others feel welcome. But, if this is something you struggle with personally, one way to correct it is to try. Make an effort the next time you see a visitor. You don't have to share your life's story. A friendly "Hello" and "It's great to see you!" will suffice.

Any congregation which is not necessarily as warm as they ought to be must be taught and trained over a period of time to "think on these things" so they might increase their joy in the presence of the Lord.

Unity Must Exist Within the Congregation

Unity is defined as: a being united; oneness; harmony; agreement; a union of related parts; a harmonious, unified arrangement of parts in an artistic work; continuity of purpose, action, etc. (Webster's New World Dictionary).

Some synonyms of unity include: oneness, wholeness, fusion, merger, confederation, federation, friendship, fellowship, and like-mindedness (Roget's Thesaurus).

A congregation must stand fast in one spirit, with one mind, striving together for the faith of the gospel (Philippians 1:27).

Unity is essential to eternal life. To inherit eternal life, we must be of one mind, having compassion on each other, and loving each other as brethren (1Peter 3:8-9).

Some antonyms of unity include: independence, individuality, isolation, division, separation, discord, disharmony, enmity, and ill will (*ibid.*).

We are commanded not to be desirous of vain glory, provoking one another or envying one another (Galatians 5:26). Nothing should be done through strife or vain glory.

Instead, in lowliness of mind, we should esteem each other greater than ourselves (Philippians 2:3). No division is permitted within a congregation of the Lord's people (1 Corinthians 1:10).

Congregational unity was a major theme in the writings of Paul. One can study the unity Paul had in mind from Ephesians 4:1-6. Therein we learn:

♦ We Must Have the Same Calling (v.1).

Man is called by the gospel (2 Thessalonians 2:14). Man is called to "walk worthy" of his calling (see also Colossians 1:10; 1 Thessalonians 2:12; Philippians 1:27). There can never be true unity in the body of Christ if its members are living immoral lives.

♦ We Must Have the Same Love One for Another (vv.2-3)

You might say that Paul has given us the "Beatitudes of Christian Unity" in these verses: Be Lowly (v.2); Be Meek; Be Longsuffering; Be Forbearing in Love; Be Endeavoring to keep unity (v.3).

To endeavor to "keep the unity of the Spirit in the bond of peace" is to be eager, or be diligent to be united and at peace with each other.

♦ We Must Have a Likeminded Faith and Love for the Teachings of the Scriptures (vv.4-6).

Paul lists several fundamental concepts upon which Christians should be united. One Body (the church), One Spirit, One Hope (v.4); One Lord, One Faith, One Baptism (v.5); One God and Father (v.6).

133

We learn from this passage that there is a practical, personal aspect of church unity and there is a doctrinal aspect to church unity. Unity does not occur in spite of our behavior but because of it. Likewise, unity will not come in spite of doctrine, but because of it.

Care about the Future of the Church

Each congregation is responsible for its future. We choose the direction we are going to travel. We can choose to be alive *in name only* (Revelation 3:1); or we can choose to be an example to all believers (1Thessalonians 1:5-8). We can grow and be alive together or we can die together. Either way, the responsibility is upon the shoulders of each congregation.

To speak of the future of the church is to speak about the young people and children. Children are what you expect them to be. Have high expectations for your children! Expect them to be faithful Christians. Expect them to be outstanding citizens. Expect them to excel in the classroom and/or workplace. Let them know that these things are expected.

Perhaps the greatest hope we have for the children in this country is for Christian parents to raise their children in such a way as not to be affected by evil environments, but to affect their environments for good, for Christ, and His gospel! Train them to meet the devil on the Lord's terms and help them to build a faith that will lead them to victory!

To care about the future of the church is to take ownership in what you are doing. The future of the Lord's church at my home congregation depends on me. I am going to examine myself and see what I am doing to bring about a bright future for my home congregation.

Having examined self, I will determine to live each day 1% better and more faithfully than yesterday. If everyone will do this, we will secure a bright future for the Lord's church.

Be Optimistic When Planning for the Future

As we have discussed in previous chapters, optimism is a key to church growth. It is essential to our success that we have the right attitude.

We need to have the faith of Joshua and Caleb who believed in the promises of God and knew they could take the Promised Land. Remember, if a congregation or its leadership has the mentality of the "one talent man" any hope for growth will be buried and left for dead!

Basically one-half of this study has been spent to convince you that the church can grow. We can be everything God wants us to be. We can thrive as His children and bring forth much fruit. The key is for each member to believe such can be done and work toward that end. Each one, reach one.

In Conclusion

For a congregation to grow, some basic needs must be met. In this lesson, we have discussed a handful of such needs. Our next lesson will be the continuation and conclusion to this portion of our study.

"Peace be to the brethren, and love with faith, from God the Father and the Lord Jesus Christ. Grace be with all them that love our Lord Jesus Christ in sincerity. Amen" (Ephesians 6:23-24).

Discussion Questions for Chapter Twelve

1.) Discuss what it means to have balance in your congregation.

2.) Discuss the importance of having a faithful, biblical eldership. What are some things you can do to encourage your elders?

3.) Discuss the importance of unity in your home congregation.

4.) What are some ideas which can be implemented to promote unity, concern for the future, and optimism in your home congregation?

13
Basic Needs for Church Growth (Part Two)

In our previous lesson we discussed five basic needs for church growth. The present lesson will serve as the continuation and conclusion of that lesson. Let us now conclude by addressing five additional needs for true church growth.

Use the Youth in the Work

We live in a time when an estimated one-third of our young people are leaving the church. The only way to reverse this trend is for Christian parents to determine to see their children put away youthful lusts and learn how to work for the Lord (Proverbs 22:6; Ephesians 6:2). Parents and children of such faith do exist and churches should feel privileged to use their Christian youth in the work.

We have the examples of David, Timothy, and Mark because adults were willing to let them work. While being young they learned to give their lives to God. They grew from being young people who knew how to work for the Lord into adults who knew how to work for the Lord.

The need to be evangelistic should be stressed to our youth at an early age. Evangelism begins at home. If it is important to the parents, it will stand a better chance of being important to the children.

If our children are raised to believe that being a Christian revolves around worship services and attending Bible classes, we have failed them. The Christian religion is an everyday religion; and every day presents to us new opportunities to be evangelistic.

Lessons for Our Youth from Ecclesiastes 11:9-12:1, 13

"Rejoice, O young man, in thy youth; and let thy heart cheer thee in the days of thy youth, and walk in the ways of thine heart, and in the sight of thine eyes: but know thou, that for all these things God will bring thee into judgment. Therefore remove sorrow from thy heart, and put away evil from thy flesh: for childhood and youth are vanity. Remember now thy Creator in the days of thy youth, while the evil days come not, nor the years draw nigh, when thou shalt say, I have no pleasure in them…" (Ecclesiastes 11:9-12:1)

"Let us hear the conclusion of the whole matter: Fear God, and keep his commandments: for this is the whole duty of man" (Ecclesiastes 12:13).

Every young person must understand that they too have the responsibility of making right decisions. While a youth can choose to follow those things that allure the eyes and feelings (Ecclesiastes 12:9), he must know that God will judge both young and old alike for their evil decisions (Ecclesiastes11:9).

Young people must put away sorrow and evil in their youth and give their lives to God. By so doing, they will have a solid foundation for this life and the life to come (Ecclesiastes11:10-12:1). Help them to learn to overcome peer pressure while young and begin doing right from an early age; for this will lead to victory over evil temptations throughout the remainder of life.

Someday our spirits will return to God and we will reap what we have sown. "Then shall the dust return to the earth as it was: and the spirit shall return unto God who gave it (12:7)." Therefore, "Remember thy Creator in the days of thy youth..."

Whether we are young or old, we must, "Fear God and keep His commandments...for, this is the whole duty of man" (Ecclesiastes 12:13).

Put Available Resources to Work

People who are willing to work must be used. Use what available space is in the meeting house or elsewhere for food pantries and clothing closets for the truly needy (cf. 2 Thessalonians 3:10). Funds that are available, outside of whatever limit the elders may determine essential for emergency purposes, should be put to use rather than saved and coveted.

Oftentimes, a congregation will find most of the resources needed are resources they already had but simply were not using. In other words, don't let the church bus sit there and rust. Use it! Don't allow the books in the church library to go unread. Study! And above all, don't allow the Lord's money to sit covetously in a bank somewhere! Put it to work!

God is able and willing to bless His church and provide us with the things He deems essential to our success. "God is able to make all grace abound toward you; that ye, always having all sufficiency in all things, may abound to every good work" (2 Corinthians 9:8).

In the church, God has set everything necessary to accomplish His intentions toward saving the lost. To be a member of the Lord's church is to belong to the all-sufficient and eternally purposed family of God.

As the Scriptures are all sufficient in an informative sense of God's will, the church is all sufficient pertaining to the Christian's good works. We do not need change in God's system and strategy purposed in the church; but, we may need to change what we are doing – especially if we are not properly utilizing all of our available resources.

Operate a Solid Bible School Program

An entire chapter could be devoted to the Bible School Program of the local church. Seeing that a chapter has not been set aside for this study, let us delve deeply into it now.

➢ Bible School classes must have teachers who are knowledgeable and glad to teach.

The teachers selected must be the very finest, most faithful members in the congregation. They should easily be seen as examples to their students.

We must not over burden these fine teachers to the point that they would regret being asked to teach. Keep them fresh.

Help them to be excited about the class they are to teach by giving them a selection of subject possibilities and time to prepare.

The curriculum must be progressive and relative. A child does not need to study second grade grammar until middle school and neither should a child stay on one book or subject of the Bible for years at a time. Our children must learn about marriage before they marry, about baptism before they are young adults, and about faithfulness before it is too late.

Similar comments should be made regarding adult Bible classes. As teachers for these classes, our aim should be to keep the ball rolling and keep the class moving forward.

Adult Bible classes should be filled with rich, deep studies from God's word. However, "rich and deep" does not imply "still and slumbering." A teacher can drain all enthusiasm from a class with too much deliberation. Yet, a teacher can also frustrate those looking for a deeper study from God's word by skimming over passages which deserve deeper concentration.

No one who has ever taught an adult Bible class would disagree as to the challenge of keeping the class moving forward while at the same time delving into the text for a rich exegesis when necessary.

➤ A "New Converts" class is an exceptional idea.

New converts should also be given the opportunity to learn at a rate of speed and on a level uniquely profitable for them. If a congregation decides to offer such a class, let it be offered not only to new converts but also to other Christians who feel they need reminding of the first principles and could benefit from more elementary studies in the Scriptures. Perhaps the title "First Principles Class" would be more suitable and less alienating than "New Converts Class."

➢ Each class should emphasize its growth.

Each class must be dedicated to recruiting new students. The Bible study program should become an instrument of growth for the congregation. From this effort, we expect to see lost souls come to know the Lord.

Time should be allotted during each session to pray for the lost, specifically those with which we are presently working. We should also be found discussing plans for visiting in the upcoming week, and even reviewing what has been done in the previous week or weeks. Allotting time each week for evangelism will keep the class aware of the emphasis we are placing on the growth of the congregation through its Bible classes and their responsibility in this cause.

➢ Time should be given to forming a *Bible School Handbook* for the congregation.

A deacon or capable member should be placed as a director of the Bible School Program. He should be someone who understands the concept of an evangelistic Bible School and the importance of sound organization, communication, and doctrine.

The work of Bible School Director is much like the work of an academic dean at a college. He should be responsible to the teachers and for the teachers. In conjunction with the elders a curriculum should be installed for child's classes as well as adult classes. The curriculum should be set in place with a variety of classes offered for adults according to available manpower.

A secretary for the Bible School Program can be appointed to organize paper work on the classes and recruiting records. Teachers and substitute teachers should be recruited and teacher prospects should be trained adequately. Hold monthly meetings just for the teachers to come together and discuss their prospect lists and those with whom they are working and recruiting for their Bible classes.

➤ Train new teachers.

Allow Bible teachers to have a teacher's helper who is there to help and learn how the class should be conducted. By so doing, you will be using your best teachers to teach and to train simultaneously.

➤ What are we expecting to accomplish with the Bible School Program?

What are our intentions? Are we having Bible classes simply for the sake of saying we have them? Is our primary purpose to offer classes for children and, therefore, we offer classes to the parents who bring the children? Are we hoping to provide spiritual growth and continued Bible education for those who are already Christians? Or, do we want to provide a Bible education to all while using this opportunity to train our people to be soul-winners and reach out to the lost? What is our objective?

In many places the importance of the Bible School Program has diminished. The attitude seems to be that as long as we have teachers willing to teach, and a workbook for them to teach from, all is well. We can do so much more! We can improve. But, where do we begin?

It begins with recognition. The church must recognize that God intends for His church to serve as His educational institution on this earth. We are God's educational system.

It is the responsibility of the local church to educate her members in all the words of life – including the doctrine of personal evangelism. We must also recognize that our responsibility does not end with educating members. We must also serve as God's educational institution in teaching the lost.

Having come to this recognition of our place and responsibility in the world, we must desire to be obedient to God in His purposes for us. The Savior said, "If you love me, you will keep my commandments." Now, out of our love for Him, let us make disciples. In order to make disciples we must organize. In other words, we cannot afford to go about a work as important as this haphazardly. Let us form a plan, set goals, and go to work.

You will only get out of people what you expect. If you expect to have a mediocre or average Bible school program, committed to attendance only and "fill-in the blank" answers – that is all you will have. But, who wants to be average? Should we not desire to be excellent? Should we not strive to be like the churches of Macedonia (2 Corinthians 8; 1 Thessalonians 1) who went above and beyond what was expected of them?

Why not expect excellence out of your congregation and its Bible School Program? Why not expect your teachers and students to be evangelistic and recruiting students? If all you expect is their attendance, their attendance is the most you will get. Why not use this time – at least part of it – to train the students and discuss plans for further evangelistic efforts?

If you expect the minimum you will see minimal effort. Let us expect the most out of our members and help them by training them unto the greatest possible good.

We should expect the most out of our teachers. Teaching God's word is a sacred responsibility. Being selected to teach God's word in the Bible school program is a tremendous honor.

As teachers, we must take this responsibility and the trust with which it is given seriously, knowing that the salvation of the souls of our loved ones depends upon our willingness to teach them the truth of God's word.

A *Bible School Handbook* will provide the teachers, students, and parents of students a clear picture of your Bible School Program, including the qualifications for teachers, expectations, goals, organization, procedure, and curriculum. It will to ensure the finest and best possible Bible school program for everyone.

We should want to see our Bible schools grow. Moreover, we should desire to see every teacher and student advance in their growth in the "grace and knowledge of the Lord" (2 Peter 3:18).

To enjoy such growth will demand hard work, dedication, and sacrifice. Above all, it will require our willingness to "seek first the kingdom and His righteousness" (Matthew

6:33). We should pray that our Bible School Program will be pleasing to God. If it is pleasing to Him, we trust it will be pleasing to a God-fearing congregation of His people.

We should expect the same dedication from our students enrolled in the Bible School Program. Nothing would be wrong with requiring sound, supplementary reading. To the contrary, it would be beneficial to the students if it was the right material.

Why not assign work for the students to do away from the classroom? Such work would include visiting the sick and wayward, setting up Bible study appointments, and executing the study itself. Homework could be assigned to the younger classes. Classes could also be offered to train preachers and teachers with necessary requirements being placed. You will get out of people only that which you expect of them. Let us expect of one another only that which God expects of each of us – our very best.

By applying the following objectives, a congregation will establish its expectations for the Bible School and clearly present what the leaders are hoping to accomplish and provide for the best possible learning experience and environment for all who are involved. Objectives should include but are not limited to the following:

1.) Use the Lord's treasury wisely in supplying the necessary tools and supplies required.

2.) Use the best and most capable teachers in the Bible school program.

148

3.) Use the faithful teachers we are blessed to have in training and developing faithful Bible teachers for coming generations.

4.) Use Bible School enrollment as a key factor in bringing lost souls to Christ.

5.) Use the Bible School in an effective way by following up with visitors, even visiting children and their parents, by using a plan and study enacted for setting private Bible study appointments.

6.) Offer as wide a variety of classes, subject matter, and diversity among teacher styles as possible to educate adults better without becoming bogged down for years at a time in one particular study.

7.) Provide a setting conducive to learning with a comfortable, relaxed, non-threatening atmosphere allowing the students to feel comfortable to discuss the Scriptures in a free-flowing way.

8.) Offer adult classes conducive to adult education with the students learning to study and interpret the Scriptures for themselves and a great deal of open discussion occupying our class time.

9.) Provide adults with the opportunity to grow spiritually through our Bible School Program to the degree that they have become capable teachers, possible preachers, and greater personal evangelists.

10.) Offer a "first principles" class perpetually for those who have recently obeyed the gospel to continue learning at their own speed or those who are visiting and have yet to obey the gospel.

Do we need to renew our commitment to the Bible school program? Are we doing our very best to make it the very best learning experience? Many times in life we are faced with the opportunity to stop and examine what we are doing. Perhaps now is an appropriate time for our home congregation to exercise this judgment and closely evaluate our Bible School.

Whatever we do for God must be done with the hope of accomplishing the greatest possible good. Let us pray and work for the education of the saved and lost alike through our Bible School Program.

Stay Engaged in Good Works

Ira North used to say, "A going church is a growing church." May we never grow tired of going! We will reap in due season if we faint not (Galatians 6:9).

Be assured and comforted by Paul's exhortation and knowing that our labor is not in vain in the Lord (1 Corinthians 15:58). Growth may not come overnight, but it will come *if* we remain steadfast and vigilant in our preaching of the gospel and promoting of the risen Savior. The congregation that tells about all they *used* to do is the selfsame congregation that will lament when speaking of how many members they *used* to have.

The Christian religion is a proactive religion. It is a religion that requires going and doing. We must go and we must do. We must take the initiative. Rather than waiting for the lost to come to us, we must go to them.

Remain Faithful to God

If we hope to grow, we must follow God's instructions. The Lord will work through us and add to His church when the seed has been sown and watered. Apart from the Lord, a congregation is merely a severed branch without hope or life (John 15:1-6).

Church growth is a blessing given by almighty God. Men do not add to the Lord's church. Men are added to the Lord's church by God. Only when we are faithful in preaching and teaching the gospel will souls have a true opportunity to be saved by obeying the gospel.

Our faith should glorify God (Romans 4:20). Our faith should be a blessing to others (James 2:14-18). Our faith should be pleasing to God (Hebrews 11:6).

In Conclusion

If we should choose not to be faithful to God by preaching the unadulterated gospel of Christ, we will be found guilty of breaking our covenant with Him. The Lord has promised to add souls to the church on the stipulated condition that the church teaches the gospel so that sinners might obey. We must keep this covenant, if the church is to grow.

God has decreed that no soul shall be saved apart from repentance and obedience to His plan of salvation (Acts 17:30; 2 Peter 3:9; Hebrews 5:8-9). He will provide increase only upon the sowing and watering of the seed of the kingdom which is His word (1 Corinthians 3:6-7). God will not break His word (Titus 1:2).

If we choose not to teach the gospel, God will not provide increase. If we choose to share the gospel, God will bless us. He alone has stipulated these terms for church growth.

Let us humble ourselves beneath His mighty hand, and determine to accomplish the mission He has set before us with faithfulness. Only through the faithfulness of God will His faithful church be exalted unto an eternal glory.

"Humble yourselves therefore under the mighty hand of God, that he may exalt you in due time: Casting all your care upon him; for he careth for you. Be sober, be vigilant; because your adversary the devil, as a roaring lion, walketh about, seeking whom he may devour: Whom resist stedfast in the faith, knowing that the same afflictions are accomplished in your brethren that are in the world. But the God of all grace, who hath called us unto his eternal glory by Christ Jesus, after that ye have suffered a while, make you perfect, stablish, strengthen, settle you. To him be glory and dominion for ever and ever. Amen" (1 Peter 5:6-11).

Discussion Questions for Chapter Thirteen

1.) Discuss some ways the youth could be used in the work of your home congregation. How can you better equip young Christians to save souls?

2.) What are some of the suggestions that have been made in this study that could make your Bible School more evangelistic and more effective?

3.) Discuss the importance of organization and expectations in the Bible School Program.

4.) What are you currently hoping to accomplish with your Bible School Program?

Part Two: Personal Evangelism

14
What Is Personal Evangelism?

In the second part of this study we shall be focusing on personal evangelism. We will begin our study of this theme by defining the subject. Once the subject is clearly set before us, we hope to offer encouragement to the reader to be a soul winner through personal evangelism. Finally, we will provide some specifics for specific situations which can help to prepare the reader for encounters and studies one may have.

The purpose of this lesson is not to cover any uncharted ground, but to remind the reader of things possibly forgotten or simply set aside. When we discuss personal evangelism, we discuss a subject that is absolutely essential to the health and growth of the Lord's church at large and in any given community.

What Is Personal Evangelism?

To define personal evangelism adequately, let us begin by asking, what is evangelism? Possibly the simplest and most agreeable definition is that evangelism is teaching the Lord's word to others. Evangelism is sowing and watering the seed of the kingdom.

Understanding this will help us to see how evangelism is necessary for church growth. As we have studied, God gives increase to the church through evangelism – the sowing and watering of His seed. Just as a farmer cannot harvest without sowing and watering seed, a church cannot increase without sowing and watering seed – the seed of the kingdom.

What then is personal evangelism? Perhaps we can all agree that personal evangelism is taking church growth – this sowing and watering concept – personally.

Let us not take personal evangelism lightly. It is a command (Mark 16:15). And, as we obey this command, Christ has promised He will be with us to ensure our success (Mark 16:20).

Seeing that evangelism is a command, every Christian (male and female) should be found obeying. We should grow and mature to the point in our spirituality that we are able, ready, and even zealous in our desire to teach the lost.

Yet, we often treat this command as if it were optional; or we look upon it with woeful dread as a child complaining about his chores. Personal evangelism should not be dreaded, but understood as absolutely essential to the growth of the church and the salvation of lost souls.

For one who earnestly desires to do the will of God, there is no getting around the necessity of personal evangelism. Whatever our calling is in life, let us be found teaching and sharing the wonderful story of love. Let us be found using the unique abilities and talents we each have to work together and bring the lost to Christ.

We each have a circle of influence. This circle is comprised of friends, relatives, neighbors, and even visitors to our assemblies. The goal we will set forth is for us to be faithful within this circle of influence by winning souls for Christ. Each one, reach one.

Personal Evangelism Is Mirroring the Light of God

Personal evangelism is serving others. Paul wrote, "For we preach not ourselves, but Christ Jesus the Lord; and ourselves your servants for Jesus' sake" (2 Corinthians 4:5). Paul continued by saying that God has "shone in our hearts to give the light of the knowledge of the glory of God in the face of Christ Jesus" (v.6).

Our light does not emanate from within ourselves; but it is a reflective light. Our hearts are a mirror for the light of God. As God's light shines upon our hearts, we reflect His light to the world so that they might know "the light of the knowledge of the glory of God."

Whatever our station is in life, we ought to have this type of servant's mentality. God is calling us to share our knowledge of Christ. He is shining His light upon us so that we can reflect this light to the world. Our lives become a mirror for God's light as we mirror the image of Christ.

Personal Evangelism Is Listening

Personal evangelism involves listening. To quote a former professor, Leon Estep, "Listening is the heart of personal evangelism." His point was, as teachers of the gospel, we want people to open up to us. When people decide to open up to us, it is because trust has been established.

As we listen to others, we demonstrate a sincere interest in their concerns. Jesus was the Master at teaching because He was the Master at listening. He did not come making judgments on appearance, or what others were saying (see Isaiah 11:3). He taught and saved the lost because He was first trusted by those whom He taught.

In the case of the woman at the well (John 4), trust was established due in large part to Jesus' willingness to listen and reply based upon what was being said. We must follow Christ in this way as well.

Consider the value of listening in this light, would you continue seeing a doctor who never listened to you? Could you ever trust such a doctor? Honestly, if you felt like your doctor cared less about your concerns and simply shrugged off everything you said as being insignificant and pointless, would you continue visiting that doctor for medical treatment?

Likewise, do we honestly believe a person is going to trust us in a Bible study and continue to come to us for help if we refuse to listen to his or her concerns? Listening is essential to healthy relationships in every walk of life. Why think otherwise with regard to healthy Bible studies?

A Bible study must never be one-sided. We want people to feel like they can talk to us and connect with us. Knowing that not every person will obey the gospel after one study, would it not be essential to conduct that one study in a way that would lead to a second and possibly a third study?

Successful Bible studies do not always end in an immediate baptism. Many times we will find that a person will want to take some time to deliberate and consider conscientiously their decision before obeying the gospel. A Bible study that leads to such deliberation is indeed a successful study. God must be obeyed sincerely from the heart and obediently from the Bible (Romans 6:17). We should want every person we study with to obey God in this divinely stipulated way.

At other times, we may find that a person is simply not ready to react obediently to the message they have received and understood to be true. At times, we may study with ones who simply are not spiritually mature enough to accept the truth. Such cases could still be considered successful Bible studies if the truth is taught and if the study is concluded with both parties remaining on good terms.

If the soul with whom we have studied is not ready to obey, for whatever reason, we want to be the first person they call when they finally become ready. We can be that trusted person to lost souls by allowing them to communicate to us and by listening to their concerns during the few occasions we have to help them.

But, let us remember always the value of truth in such studies. We must never shy away from teaching the truth simply for the sake of remaining on speaking terms with an individual. Let us speak the truth in love always, but if that person is determined to despise us for teaching truth, so be it.

I have encountered studies wherein it was hard to listen to the poison being spoken. I have heard persons defy God, slap the church, gossip, and point fingers – even at me! Quite frankly, it comes with the job. It is hard to listen to such people and it is hard to care for their concerns when they are either frivolous, sinful, or both; but we must do our best.

Sometimes a person will not be satisfied until you say what the person wants to hear. To do so would mean compromising the truth of God's word; and this must never be done. In such cases, we should listen carefully to what the person is saying; repeat what we understand was said so that there is no misunderstanding; and upon making sure that we have heard correctly and repeated correctly, provide God's truth on the subject.

We cannot make decisions for lost souls. All we can do, and all we are called to do, is to present them with the truth of God's word and encourage them to obey Him.

Personal Evangelism Is Using our Knowledge, Skill, and Motivation to Succeed in Winning Souls

Knowledge, skill, and motivation – each point is equally essential to soul winning. Peter connected these three aspects of soul winning in 1 Peter 3:15.

"But sanctify the Lord God in your hearts: and be ready always to give an answer to every man that asketh you a reason of the hope that is in you with meekness and fear."

We are able to teach because of knowledge. We can answer (*apologia* – a defense of the gospel) with meekness and respect because of skill. We are ready always because we are motivated. Only by such knowledge, skill, and motivation will we succeed as soul winners.

We can know the Bible through and through, but if we are not motivated to share it, or if we cannot or will not share it with the right skill, our knowledge will be useless to others. Our ultimate motivation as faithful Christians and servants of God should be to help others come to know the salvation we know in Christ.

The only alternative to eternal salvation is eternal damnation (Matthew 25:46). As soul winners, we must believe hell is a real place. The lost will ultimately spend a never-ending eternity in hell (cf. Revelation 14:12).

As soul winners we must also believe in the hope of heaven. We want others to share in this hope and someday this reality. What more motivation do we need to share the gospel with the lost?

Personal Evangelism Is Helping People to See Their Condition in the Mirror of the Soul

Personal evangelism is helping lost souls to see themselves as they truly appear to God. To accomplish such inward self-examination will no doubt require considerable skill and knowledge of the word.

The word of God is the mirror of the soul (James 1:18-25). We must look into the word of God with a view to our own lives, actions, and ambitions. What do we see when we judge ourselves from the word of God? What needs improving? What is God requiring of me? Where do I begin?

The word of our Lord will be the standard for our final judgment (John 12:48). The Bible will read the same on the judgment day as it reads today.

Take this book you are studying. You are reading a revision of the first edition. Many words have been changed, removed, and added for clarity and improvement. But, the word of God cannot be made clearer by addition or subtraction. Such treatment of the Bible would be an injurious sin.

Our duty is not to change the word of God, but to allow it to change us. Rather than looking into the word with contempt in our hearts, we ought to seek God's favor by receiving His word with meekness and conforming to His holy will.

Likewise, when having Bible studies with lost souls, our duty is not to judge the persons with whom we study improperly, but allow them to see the word of God and rightfully judge their own condition on the basis of what they have learned.

Personal evangelism is not debating. Sometimes, however, these two concepts intertwine. At times, we can study with others who like to debate when discussing the Bible, or any topic for that matter. They may like to exchange arguments and answers. However, as personal evangelists, when we see such an exchange becoming heated, we should be quick to calm emotions in an attempt to leave the study in as good a place as possible.

The soul with whom we are studying may not be spiritually mature enough at that time to hear and heed the gospel. However, this does not mean that dear soul will never be ready to hear and obey. If and when the day arrives and they have become ready, we want to be the first one they consider contacting.

In Conclusion

It is believed that the average congregation numbers around one hundred members. It is also believed that the average congregation averages seven baptisms per year. Of these baptisms, five result from the work of the preacher; one is due to the work of the eldership; and one is from the work of everyone else in that congregation combined!

How shall we respond to this call for a greater emphasis and more obedience in personal evangelism? Will we continue dreading the thought? Or, possibly we might feel guilty for the things we have failed to do?

One thing is for sure, we must not continue going through the motions of lukewarm religion. We can continue parking in the same place, sitting in the same seat, hearing the same sermons, praying the same prayers, only to be dismissed at the same time, and return home or to the local restaurant the same way we always have.

Yes, we could surely grow old together. We will also die together; and the congregation will die with us.

The Lord's church cannot survive in any community without evangelism. Without evangelism, it is only a matter of time until the mortality rate catches up and the doors close. The worst mistake any of us can make is to do nothing at all.

By God's grace, we can become better servants and personal evangelists. As Christians, let us accept our responsibility, obey the Lord and take hope in believing the best days for the Lord's church are yet to come! Take up the cross and follow Him! Heed what He says! Do what He wills!

Finally, brethren, when our appointed time comes to travel through that valley which divides time from eternity, may we behold the glad dawn of an endless day having done all to stand! Let us find our shade beneath the tree of life and rest from the labors of this life with kindred spirits who have gone on before.

In that day, may we realize the greatness of the cause to which we were devoted and forever rejoice in the encompassing presence of those with whom we shared the unsearchable riches of the glorious gospel of Christ! *O to be a soul winner!*

"The Lord is my portion, saith my soul; therefore will I hope in him. The Lord is good unto them that wait for him, to the soul that seeketh him" (Lamentations 3:24-25).

Discussion Questions for Chapter Fourteen

1.) What is personal evangelism?

2.) Discuss the importance of listening in a Bible study.

3.) How should we respond to the person who would have us compromise the word of God in our study with them?

4.) Discuss the importance of knowledge, skill, and, motivation.

5.) Discuss the importance of judging ourselves from the word of God.

15
Jesus Was a Soul Winner

In 1892 J.G. Dailey published a gospel song now found in most hymnals titled, "Why Did My Savior Come to Earth?"

Jesus came to earth for no other reason than to save souls. He accomplished this mission. To His Father, Christ prayed: "I have glorified thee on the earth: I have finished the work which thou gavest me to do" (John 17:4).

To follow Christ is to keep His mission alive. One cannot be a follower of Christ and refuse to take part in the mission of Christ. The two are inseparable. "The disciple is not above his master: but every one that is perfect shall be as his master" (Luke 6:40).

Jesus, the great soul winner, has commanded us to keep His mission alive. "Go ye, and make disciples."

The Offer of Reconciliation

The primary reason for Christ's coming to earth was to reconcile a lost and dying creation to God. This reconciliation provides man with a renewed fellowship with God, redemption, and all spiritual blessings.

Understanding the concept of reconciliation is of utmost to soul winning. "God has reconciled us to Himself through Christ Jesus" (2 Corinthians 5:18). We are not reconciling

God to ourselves; but God is reconciling us to Himself. We are the violators and He is the forgiver in this relationship.

Forgiveness is granted only in Christ Jesus. Thus we have a ministry of reconciliation as ambassadors for Christ, in which we plead with the lost to be reconciled to God through Him (2 Corinthians 5:19-21).

Our Savior did not come only to reconcile or save one certain race or people, but the obedient of every race and all nations (Matthew 28:18-20; Mark 16:15-16; Luke 24:47).

Paul wrote: "But now, in Christ Jesus, ye who sometimes were far off are made nigh by the blood of Christ. For he is our peace, who hath made both one, and hath broken down the middle wall of partition between us... that he might reconcile both unto God in one body by the cross..." (Ephesians 2:13-17).

Again Paul wrote: "And, having made peace through the blood of his cross, by him to reconcile all things to himself; by him, I say, whether they be things in earth, or things in heaven" (Colossians 1:20).

In Christ, all men can be saved, "For the Son of Man has come to seek and save that which was lost" (Luke 19:10). And, "He, by the grace of God should taste death for every man" (Hebrews 2:9).

Again, "For therefore we both labor and suffer reproach, because we trust in the living God, who is the Savior of all men, specially of those that believe" (1 Timothy 4:10).

Jesus came to earth to be the Savior of all men. The great tragedy of life and even the burden of personal evangelism is knowing that everyone *could* be saved, because this is why our Savior came, and yet, many more will be lost than will be saved (Matthew 7:13-14). As for those who choose not to obey, although Christ died for them, because of their disobedience they will ultimately be lost (2 Thessalonians 1:7-10).

The Provision of Reconciliation

Christ provides reconciliation to "whosoever will" (Revelation 22:17) through His three-fold sacrifice. We have already learned from Paul that this reconciliation can come only by way of the cross. Yet, His death was only one aspect of our Lord's sacrifice. For Jesus to die that cruel death, He first had to leave the splendor of Heaven (Philippians 2:5-8); and He had to take on the form of a servant and come to this world as a mortal man (Hebrews 2:17). Jesus was truly the Son of God and the Son of man. After these two initial sacrifices were made by our Lord, He offered the ultimate sacrifice by being crucified and slain at the hands of wicked men (Acts 2:23).

Christ's sacrifice was all sufficient and perfect. The writer of Hebrews asks: "How much more shall the blood of Christ, who through the eternal Spirit offered himself without spot to God, purge your conscience from dead works to serve the living God?" (Hebrews 9:14)

The writer further attests to the all sufficient sacrifice of Christ by saying: "By the which will we are sanctified through the offering of the body of Jesus Christ once for all. And every priest standeth daily ministering and offering oftentimes the same sacrifices, which can never take away sins:

171

But this man, after he had offered one sacrifice for sins for ever, sat down on the right hand of God; From henceforth expecting till his enemies be made his footstool. For by one offering he hath perfected for ever them that are sanctified." (Hebrews 10:10-14).

If this world lasts for one trillion years from now, there will never be another offering needed to forgive a single sin. Just think of all the sins you are capable of committing in a single day. Now multiply that by the billions of souls alive each day. Now multiply that by infinity and you will begin to appreciate the all sufficiency of the sacrifice of Christ.

This world will never need another Savior. His one sacrifice is powerful and effective enough to cleanse every sin ever committed or to be committed for ever and ever. "Now where remission of these is, there is no more offering for sin" (Hebrews 10:18).

Jesus came to minister and give His life a ransom for many (Mark 10:45). For us to keep this mission alive we must minister by informing the world of this ransom for sin that was given once and for all by the grace of almighty God.

The Requirements for Reconciliation

Jesus not only came to die for us, and thus reconcile us to His Father, He also came to preach the gospel and make His plan known. Just as the offer is from God, so are the terms. To win souls, Jesus had to reveal the terms of salvation.

The gospel includes the terms of reconciliation. The gospel is the doctrine that must be obeyed from the heart (see

Romans 6:17-18). By obeying this gospel, one becomes reconciled to God through the cross of Christ. It would be futile to try to sever the gospel from the cross or from the reconciliation being offered. The gospel makes known to us the offer as well as the terms of the offer.

When Jesus returned to Nazareth, He went into the synagogue on the Sabbath and proclaimed: "The Spirit of the Lord is upon me, because he hath anointed me to preach the gospel to the poor; he hath sent me to heal the broken-hearted, to preach deliverance to the captives, and recovering the sight of the blind, to set at liberty them that are bruised, to preach the acceptable year of the Lord" (Luke 4:18-19).

Jesus was making His intentions known. He was stating His mission as a soul winner. He made His intentions known again to those who sought Him while He was in a desert place saying, "I must preach the kingdom of God to other cities also: for therefore am I sent." (Luke 4:43). The mission of Christ includes preaching the kingdom of Christ. You cannot have one without the other.

The mission of Christ involves calling sinners to repentance. We must compel them to turn from their sins unto the living God. Jesus spoke thusly, "They that are whole need not a physician; but they that are sick. I came not to call the righteous, but sinners to repentance." (Luke 5:31-32).

During the mockery of His trial, Jesus made known to Pilate His mission was to preach and bear witness to the truth. Observe:

173

"Thou sayest that I am a king. To this end was I born, and for this cause came I into the world, that I should bear witness of the truth. Every one that is of the truth heareth my voice" (John 18:37).

Our Role as Soul Winners

At this point in our study it would be beneficial to study 2 Corinthians 5:18-21 more carefully. Here's the passage: "And all things are of God, who hath reconciled us to himself by Jesus Christ, and hath given to us the ministry of reconciliation; To wit, that God was in Christ, reconciling the world unto himself, not imputing their trespasses unto them; and hath committed unto us the word of reconciliation. Now then we are ambassadors for Christ, as though God did beseech you by us: we pray you in Christ's stead, be ye reconciled to God. For he hath made him to be sin for us, who knew no sin; that we might be made the righteousness of God in him."

You will observe that Christians have a "ministry of reconciliation." Of course, we also call this the "Great Commission."

Our job is to go into the world as ambassadors for Christ, representing Him and speaking on His behalf. We are to plead and implore men to be saved by the blood of Christ.

We are to preach the very message Jesus preached. We are to preach a message of repentance and entrance in the kingdom. We are to help men to be reconciled to God by coming to Christ.

However, it is not enough for men to hear Christ from us; they must see Christ in us. Jesus took His goodness into the heart of evil, and took our evil upon Him, so that He might destroy its power. He was rich, and yet became poor, so that the poor might become rich.

The Word was made alive by becoming flesh. The Word became a living Epistle so that we might know God and be saved. It is through this Flesh that mortal man contacts the Spirit of God, and the blind are made to see, while the deaf are made to hear.

It is true that "no man ever spoke like this" and that "the people heard Him gladly." But Jesus also "went about doing good." While our Lord did a great many miracles for which we have not the power, He also did a great many good deeds for which we do have the power, and in the spirit of Christ we must "go and do likewise."

I am reminded of a story concerning a missionary in India who was rather poor with his finances and book-keeping. Finally, his brethren decided to replace him with a better book-keeper. This missionary did not quit, however, and decided to go into the remote places of that country and continue his ministry.

Years later, another missionary also went deep into the jungles and came unto a remote village. This missionary attempted to explain Christ to the people by telling of His love for the poor, how He helped the sick, and visited in their homes.

The people answered by saying, "We know him well; he has been living here for years!" The missionary who was so poor in his book-keeping had settled there and lived among them!

When the people heard the description of Christ, their minds immediately went to the man who had come to live among them, ministered to them, and cared for them. In the man who could not keep his books, the people had recognized Jesus.

May the world also recognize Christ in us! Christ must ever live in our hearts, and be seen in our deeds, if we are truly to be His ambassadors to the lost.

In Conclusion

Our Savior came to earth to make something marvelous and wonderful out of people who would otherwise be lost and destitute of hope. Jesus came to save our souls both now and forever.

Upon His ascension into the heavenly places, our Lord entrusted His church with the sacred responsibility of keeping His mission alive. As followers of Jesus, let us desire to follow Him in the great work of saving souls. Let us allow the Lord to have His influence upon us. Let us win souls in the Name which reigns eternally in our hearts.

"Now then we are ambassadors for Christ, as though God did beseech you by us: we pray you in Christ's stead, be ye reconciled to God" (2 Corinthians 5:20).

Discussion Questions for Chapter Fifteen

1.) Explain the concept of reconciliation.

2.) What was the mission of Christ?

3.) Can one be faithful to Christ without keeping His mission alive?

4.) Discuss our role as ambassadors for Christ. What is an ambassador?

5.) Discuss the importance of Christ living in us.

16
Faithful Christians Win Souls

"The fruit of the righteous is a tree of life; and he that wins souls is wise" (Proverbs 11:30).

Soul winning is a manifestation of godly wisdom. We can be victimized through the misguidance of earthly, sensual, devilish wisdom (James 3:14-16), or we can live victoriously through the guidance and gift (James 1:5) of godly wisdom (James 3:13, 17-18).

God has made the wisdom of this world look foolish when compared to the wisdom He bestows through the knowledge of His Son.

"For it is written, I will destroy the wisdom of the wise, and will bring to nothing the understanding of the prudent. Where is the wise? where is the scribe? where is the disputer of this world? hath not God made foolish the wisdom of this world... But of him are ye in Christ Jesus, who of God is made unto us wisdom, and righteousness, and sanctification, and redemption: That, according as it is written, He that glorieth, let him glory in the Lord" (1 Corinthians 1:19-20, 30-31).

Faithful Christians Are Wise

Faithful Christians are the wisest souls I know. Can you think of anyone wiser than a truly faithful Christian? Because

179

they are truly wise people, they have built their house on the rock of obedience to the word of God (Matthew 7:24-27).

Often, we are guilty of not giving ourselves enough credit. We can often allow church slappers and naysayers to criticize us into dismay. Yet, it is my conviction that the finest people on earth are members of the Lord's church!

Moreover, if one has obeyed the certified gospel which Paul preached, he has indeed proven himself to be wise. If he is living daily by the teachings of this gospel, he is proving himself daily to remain wise.

Faithful Christians have a godly wisdom which is more precious to the future of the Lord's church than possibly any other characteristic. The challenge before us is to use this wisdom in ways which will bring souls to Christ.

Winning souls is putting to use the wisdom that is of God. "Who is a wise man and endued with knowledge among you? Let him show out of a good conversation his works with meekness of wisdom." (James 3:13).

God's people should be found using such wisdom and looking for opportunities as they present themselves to bring increase to the body of Christ. As we grow and mature in the gospel we will be found growing and maturing in godly wisdom. As we develop, we ought to be found becoming more and more active in ways to bring the lost to Christ.

We each have unique abilities and strengths. We are not all made exactly alike. However, this should not deter growth, but encourage it as we work together by using our various abilities to build up the body of Christ

180

As we teach and preach the gospel in its purest form, a sweet savor unto the Lord is offered.

"Now thanks be unto God, which always causeth us to triumph in Christ, and maketh manifest the savour of his knowledge by us in every place. For we are unto God a sweet savour of Christ, In them that are saved, and in them that perish: To the one we are the savour of death unto death; and to the other the savour of life unto life. And who is sufficient for these things? For we are not as many, which corrupt the word of God: but as of sincerity, but as of God, in the sight of God speak we in Christ" (2 Corinthians 2:14-17).

I want you to see something here: being faithful and pleasing to God is not always the same as being successful or productive as soul winners. We are a sweet savor to God in those who believe and in those who perish. The very fact that we taught them the truth is what pleases the Lord. Our faithfulness does not depend upon their reception of the truth.

Paul did all he could do and taught as many as he could teach and still only saved some in comparison to those he was unable to convert (Romans 11:14; 1 Corinthians 9:22). However, his success was not measured on the basis of who believed as compared to who disbelieved, but on the basis of whether or not the truth was preached. The same is true of us today.

We see the same point illustrated in the preaching of Noah. Noah was a righteous preacher of God who preached for one hundred and twenty years, while saving only eight souls including himself (Genesis 6:3; 1 Peter 3:20; 2 Peter 2:5). Yet, who among us would dare to say he was a failure as a preacher?

We are not going to save every person we try to reach, but we will save some. Soul winning is *not* about the numbers! It is about being faithful to God. If we are faithful to God, souls will be won by our faithfulness. If a loved one is lost, we must make sure it is because of his neglect, and not our neglect.

Allow me to remind you of one more thing in connection with this thought before we proceed. A person may not be receptive *today*, but he might be receptive *tomorrow*. Sometimes a person will think seriously about the truth you have shared for a considerable amount of time before obeying it. Just because they do not obey immediately, does not mean they will not obey eventually. Let that be our prayer in such cases.

Faithful Christians Are Motivated

Faithful Christians are motivated people. God is sanctified in their hearts (1 Peter 3:15). They are motivated and can motivate by at least two related emotions – love and fear.

Jude wrote, "And of some have compassion, making a difference: And others save with fear, pulling them out of the fire; hating even the garment spotted by the flesh" (Jude 22-23).

We must have a love for souls which can be demonstrated as we seek to save the lost by compassionate pleas. At other times, we must display our fear for the destiny of the lost as we pull and even snatch them out of the fire with a message more terrible, yet no less loving.

In view of the final judgment, Paul wrote, "Knowing therefore the terror of the Lord, we persuade men" (2 Corinthians 5:11). Love and godly fear are never separate, but are joined together as the sincere reason for our obeying and sharing the gospel.

Faithful Christians do not share the terrifying message of the reality of hell with the lost because of hatred, but because of a deep and sincere love for them, because they know every soul is precious to God, and because they believe what the Bible teaches about hell.

For an example of this truth, look to Paul's admonition concerning the erring brother in 1 Corinthians 5. Paul had two goals in mind:

1.) He wanted this man's spirit to be saved in the day of the Lord (v.5).

2.) And, he wanted the congregation to be pure and free from worldly lusts and compromise (v.6).

Truly, his love was tough love; but it was no less love. In fact he said that he wrote those things so that they "might know the love which I have more abundantly toward you" (2 Corinthians 2:4).

Faithful Christians are also motivated to serve God by the possible joys of heaven. There will be no tears in heaven (Revelation 21:4). The pure water of the river of life shall flow as clearly as crystal (Revelation 22:1), and light shall radiate from the very presence of God. The voices of all the redeemed shall blend in one accord to the Lamb that was slain and the Father whose face we shall at last see as He sits upon His glory-circled throne. How beautiful heaven must be!

We shall be "gathered unto our people." We shall be reunited with faithful family members who have gone before. As David said of his son, "I shall go to him, but he shall not return to me" (2 Samuel 12:23).

We shall be reunited with those we have brought to the Lord. Of such souls Paul wrote, "that I may rejoice in the day of Christ, that I have not run in vain, neither labored in vain" (Philippians 2:16).

We will again see, and some for the first time, all the faithful Christians who have gone on before. "Blessed are the dead which die in the Lord from henceforth: Yea, saith the Spirit, that they may rest from their labors: and their works do follow them" (Revelation 14:13). *O home of the soul!*

Faithful Christians long to hear "Well done good and faithful servant." Have you ever met a soul who did not like to be told they were appreciated and that they had done a good job? If we will finish our course, someday the Lord – the righteous Judge – will say to us "Come, ye blessed of my Father, inherit the kingdom prepared for you from the foundation of the world" (Matthew 25:34). Feeble man shall never hear a compliment as high as this which is to be uttered by the Savior of souls.

Faithful Christians Are Learning

Faithful Christians are learning people. We should learn a method of teaching that works for us. We should learn ways to use our unique abilities and strengths that would help to win souls.

We should look for ways to be productive as soul winners which will not conflict with a method our faithful elders are trying to implement. (Because unfaithful elders try to implement unscriptural methods in the name of church growth, it is necessary to endorse only the ambitions and methodology of faithful elders.)

Learn to go with the flow. Be yourself and have some fun working for the Lord. If the elders decide to get a project going, the church should have fun with it and enjoy the blessing of working together. If you go visiting, when you can, go with a friend and have lunch together. Make a day of it. Enjoy working together for the Lord.

If we are having private Bible studies, we should refrain from using rehearsed speeches that will only limit our effectiveness as soul winners. By all means have a plan in place, but don't forget to enjoy it and be yourself!

For some it is hard to make visits. Allow me to suggest something that helps me: take something with you. Take some homegrown tomatoes or a homemade pie. (Come visit me when you do!) You will find that this will take all the awkwardness out of visiting people and break the ice.

Moreover, don't feel like you have to talk about religion at the beginning of your visit. Just visit and enjoy their company and let them enjoy your company. Offer an invitation to church or a Bible study before you leave. *Listen and react* to their response.

Our ability and awareness will broaden as we continue attempting to win souls. No one should expect to be an expert teacher or soul winner before getting started. Surely no reasonable brother or sister expects this of you.

We *will* make some mistakes along the way. When we make mistakes we must remember, a mistake only means there is room for improvement – and there will always be room for improvement.

Is this not part of growing and maturing in the faith? Just think of how many potentially wonderful soul winners we know who have never tried to win souls simply because they are afraid of making a few mistakes? Let this never be true of us. Remember, the greatest mistake we can make is to do nothing.

Faithful Christians Are Forgiving

Faithful Christians are forgiving, compassionate people. They realize that everyone has sinned and that we are all in need of forgiveness. They also take to heart the Lord's teaching on the subject and realize that if they want to be forgiven, they must be willing to forgive.

I believe it goes even deeper than that. Faithful Christians forgive because of a spirit of meekness that dwells within them (Galatians 6:1-2). They know assuredly that they too were once in the place of the lost soul, and but by the grace of God, they could be again.

Moreover, they forgive because they want to be perfect, as their Father in heaven is perfect (Matthew 5:43-48). They want to forgive as He forgives (Ephesians 4:32).

186

Faithful Christians forgive others because that is the Savior's way and they are following His example (1 Peter 2:21). They want to be like Jesus, and no greater forgiver ever walked the face of the earth.

The forgiving spirit of faithful Christians helps the lost to realize that God is a forgiving God. He is rich in mercy and willing to forgive. So too are faithful Christians.

Faithful Christians Are Powerful

Faithful Christians are powerful people. Our power is in the *Man* we preach. "For we preach not ourselves, but Christ Jesus the Lord; and ourselves your servants for Jesus' sake" (2 Corinthians 4:6).

Paul also made known that our power is the *message* we preach: "For I am not ashamed of the gospel of Christ: for it is the power of God unto salvation to every one that believeth; to the Jew first, and also to the Greek. For therein is the righteousness of God revealed from faith to faith: as it is written, 'The just shall live by faith'" (Romans 1:16-17).

God has not given us a spirit of fear, but of power, love, and a sound mind (2 Timothy 1:7). Faithful Christians believe they can do all things through the strength of Christ (Philippians 4:13). They are powerful people because they choose to live in God's strength rather than their weaknesses.

They are also powerful people because they are resilient people. They may get knocked down. They may even fall. But they always get back up. For all of these reasons faithful Christians are uniquely qualified to win souls.

In Conclusion

Disappointments await, evils allure, and a powerful adversary confronts as a roaring lion. Who in their right mind would want to be a soul winner? A faithful Christian – that's who! To be remembered as a soul winner is the greatest legacy a person could leave.

Soul winners are all around us. Christian mothers who seemingly single handedly raise their children to be Christians are soul winners! Christian fathers who raise their children in the nurture and admonition of the Lord are soul winners! The carpenter who shares Christ with his buddy and co-worker during their lunch is a soul winner! Whatever our place is in life, as we go, let us go teaching the gospel (Matthew 28:18-20). Let us be found faithful in whatever opportunity we have and we will be found glorifying God.

When the time comes for us to pass into glory and rest from our labors, let us be found accepted and wise. May our eternity together be filled with rejoicing, renewed fellowship with the saints who have gone on before, and with all those precious souls whom we shared the good news and the gospel of peace!

"And they that be wise shall shine as the brightness of the firmament; and they that turn many to righteousness as the stars for ever and ever" (Daniel 12:3).

Discussion Questions for Chapter Sixteen

1.) What is the fruit of godly wisdom?

2.) What motivates a Christian to win souls?

3.) Are we "un-loving" to rebuke a person because of sin?

4.) Discuss the importance of having fun and enjoying working alongside one another in a church project.

5.) Discuss the reality of making mistakes. What is the worst mistake we can make?

6.) Who is a faithful Christian?

17
Who Among You Is Wise?

"Who is wise and understanding among you?" (James 3:13). James raised a profound question. In many instances, a stark contrast is displayed by those who are considered to be wise and their actions and ambitions. Such cases show the difference in a person who is considered to be wise and a person who truly acts with wisdom. One may be esteemed highly among his colleagues and friends in the world as being a wise person and yet remain unproven in making biblically wise decisions.

It is interesting to note that James asked, "Who is wise and understanding among *you*?" The evangelist is not instructing us to view the world and consider the actions of the supposed wise therein. Rather, our brother is teaching us about an evaluation which must be made from within the church.

Who among the brethren is wise? Let those men prove their wisdom to the brotherhood by their good conduct and works that are done in the meekness of wisdom.

In other words, we should not haphazardly praise a brother as being wise. We must listen, learn, and discern by observable actions exactly who is wise.

Moreover, we must allow God's word to be our rule in making such judgments. In observing our brethren we cannot go above and beyond that which is written (1 Corinthians

4:6). We cannot prove who is wise among us by simply comparing ourselves by ourselves. "For we dare not make ourselves of the number, or compare ourselves with some that commend themselves: but they measuring themselves by themselves, and comparing themselves among themselves, are not wise" (2 Corinthians 10:12).

The Wise Christian Obeys God

We can learn who is wise among us from their obedience to God. The Bible teaches, "The fear of the Lord is the beginning of wisdom; a good understanding have all those who do His commandments. His praise endures forever!" (Psalm 111:10).

Wise Christians will do what God has commanded. Wise Christians will fear the Lord and put this fear into practice by hating evil (Proverbs 8:13) and thus turning away from evil (Proverbs14:16).

A wise brother will not suppress the truth and yet proclaim wisdom. God's wrath shall be upon those who do so.

"For the wrath of God is revealed from heaven against all ungodliness and unrighteousness of men, who hold the truth in unrighteousness...Professing themselves to be wise, they became fools" (Romans 1:18, 22).

Obeying God is not always easy. But, God is not asking us to do what is easy all the time. He is commanding us to be faithful, even when being faithful isn't easy.

The Wise Christian Seeks Wisdom from God

The wise man asks God for wisdom (James 1:5). A wise person is wise enough to know not to lean upon his own understanding, but to look to God (Proverbs 3:5). The Lord gives wisdom (Proverbs 2:5).

The wise Christian will be careful to walk with wisdom by making the most of his time. "See then that ye walk circumspectly, not as fools, but as wise, Redeeming the time, because the days are evil" (Ephesians 5:15-16).

Wise brethren are also cautious not to return to a former way of life (Ephesians 4:17 ff.). They are ashamed of those things and realize their fruitless end (Romans 6:21).

The wise one among us is the one who respects the authority of God's word. In Proverbs 9:8, we are told, "Do not correct a scoffer, lest he hate you; rebuke a wise man, and he will love you."

A wise brother has no problem repenting when shown to be in direct conflict with the word of God. The wise man will love you for such teaching.

On the other hand, the scoffer will hate you for saying anything at all. Certainly we can relate to this pertaining to the subject of soul winning. Many times a conversation will result in hurt feelings, not because you said something wrong, but because you were attempting to teach a "scoffer."

Let us be careful never to become so high-minded that we refuse to repent when we are in the wrong. God resists the proud and gives grace to the humble (James 4:6).   May wisdom be our strength (Ecclesiastes 7:19)!

The Wise Christian Leads with Godly Wisdom

Without a doubt, we are going to be placed in difficult situations and called upon to answer difficult questions. We must "study to answer" (Proverbs 15:28) such questions. But what chance do we have when these events arise if we do not have godly wisdom?

Our congregations must be governed with godly wisdom. Our families must be led with godly wisdom. But before any of this can happen, our hearts must be directed by godly wisdom.

Solomon's prayer must become our prayer: "Give thy servant an understanding heart…" (1 Kings 3:9). However, as we also learn from Solomon, it is not enough to pray for wisdom, or even to be granted wisdom; we must live according to the wisdom God has given us.

The Wise Christian Cares Enough to Correct Error

Solomon wrote, "It is better to hear the rebuke of the wise than for man to hear the song of fools" (Ecclesiastes 7:5).

The wise man not only loves the one who corrects him when wrong, but he is also willing to correct the wrong.

Have we become too concerned with upsetting the lost to instruct them properly? Would we rather have a friend on earth over a brother in heaven? Be careful, lest this cherished friend becomes an enemy in hell for not teaching him the truth when you had the opportunity!

A wise Christian is willing to help the fallen one return from the error of his way (James 5:19). Wise Christians are willing to preach the word "in season and out of season." We are taught, "The fruit of the righteous is a tree of life, and he who wins souls is wise" (Proverbs 11:30).

In Conclusion

The reason we have spent the time we have on this subject in this study is so that we will recognize wise brethren, learn from them, and seek to become wise Christians as well. I am afraid that we listen to the wrong people too many times, when we should be ignoring them. Let us learn to appreciate godly wisdom and follow it, while also learning to dispel the criticisms and anxieties of those who are not wise.

Solomon said, "Wisdom is the principle thing; therefore get wisdom..." (Proverbs 4:7). We believe godly wisdom is principle to church growth and personal evangelism.

➢ A Christian with godly wisdom is going to fear the Lord and instruct others only according to the word of God, thus enabling the lost to obey the truth and God to add them to the church.

➢ A Christian with godly wisdom is going to seek wisdom from God. He is going to seek to understand matters pertaining to life and godliness as God has revealed them. He will be prepared to encounter any situation with wisdom from above.

> A Christian with godly wisdom is going to know what is at stake. Such a one will want to make a difference. This Christian will be found caring for the lost and attempting to lead them to the truth.

May wisdom be seen in our lives and grasped in our words. If ever there was a time for God's people to act with wisdom, it is now. As God's children, let us obey Him, seek our wisdom from Him, and be vigilant in promoting this wisdom that is from above. Let us stand united as one body, reconciled to God, believing in the power of the cross.

As wise and faithful Christians, may we be found dedicated to this noblest and highest calling! Let us fill our communities with this doctrine as did our beloved brethren in the not so long ago (Acts 5:28). Let us prove ourselves to God, our brethren, and our fellow man as being the highest quality of humankind – a wise and faithful Christian.

"O how love I thy law! it is my meditation all the day. Thou through thy commandments hast made me wiser than mine enemies: for they are ever with me. I have more understanding than all my teachers: for thy testimonies are my meditation. I understand more than the ancients, because I keep thy precepts. I have refrained my feet from every evil way, that I might keep thy word. I have not departed from thy judgments: for thou hast taught me. How sweet are. thy words unto my taste! yea, sweeter than honey to my mouth! Through thy precepts I get understanding: therefore I hate every false way" (Psalm 119:97-104).

Discussion Questions for Chapter Seventeen

1.) How can we know who among us is wise?

2.) Solomon had wisdom; but how did he fail?

3.) Discuss the importance of godly wisdom as it pertains to church growth and personal evangelism.

18
Forming and Working from a Prospect List

As we have stated, the plan we propose in this book is biblical and it will work in congregations of 20, 200, or 2000. It is simple when you think about it: "Each One Reach One." We each have a circle of influence – a circle of life, if you will. Within this circle we will find our prospects and greatest opportunities to save souls.

Paul spoke about a "sphere which God appointed us" (2 Corinthians 10:13). The goal is to increase the faith of those within our sphere; and as souls are saved, the sphere increases (v.15), and our potential for good increases.

Who among us would like to increase this circle of influence and the number of souls we and our congregation are winning for the Lord? Just as no athletic team can win consistently without a game plan, no congregation or Christian can win souls consistently without a game plan.

Sometimes our methods produce little results. A Christian can become confused at such times and lose faith in the gospel when all they truly need to do is back up, refocus, maybe redirect their thoughts, and try again with what could be a more effective method. By forming and working from a prospect list, a soul winner will have a proven biblical plan and base of operation.

Everyone knows someone who needs the gospel. By developing such a list, a Christian and a congregation will be better equipped. Two categories that should be on every prospect list are *unique prospects* and *shared prospects*.

Unique Prospects

We each have prospects unique to our lives. Examples of such prospects are family members, friends, and neighbors. Andrew had a unique prospect in mind when he told his brother Peter of the Christ (John 1:40-42).

Andrew started with his family and his first prospect was his brother. Andrew did not stop at asking or telling Peter of Jesus. Rather, Andrew *brought* Peter to Jesus. His family included a prospect for the Lord. Our families are filled with prospects for the Lord! Your prospect list should include:

- ➢ Children
- ➢ Parents
- ➢ Brothers and Sisters
- ➢ Cousins
- ➢ Grandparents
- ➢ Aunts and Uncles
- ➢ Nieces and Nephews

The demon possessed man was given a *personal commission*. Jesus told this man, "Go home to thy friends, and tell them how great things the Lord hath done for thee, and hath had compassion on thee" (Mark 5:19).

Since this man's community forbad Christ from entering, this once possessed man stood as their lone hope for accepting Christ. It could be that some of us stand as the lone hope for a few lost souls among us.

Mission work is to be done at home. Our home communities are likely filled with friends in need of the gospel whom we have probably known for considerable amounts of time. The Savior taught this man to go to such friends. His friends were prospects for Christ. Our friends are prospects for Christ!

The Samaritan woman of Sychar had in her mind the souls of her neighbors. Having encountered Jesus at Jacob's well, "The woman then left her waterpot, and went her way into the city, and saith to the men, Come, see a man, which told me all things that ever I did: is not this the Christ?" (John 4:28-29)

It appears she went unto those she knew, which certainly would have included her neighbors. Her invitation was, "Come and see."

Do you suppose we could use this same invitation today? Was she not successful in inviting her neighbors? Her neighbors were prospects for Christ. Our neighbors are prospects for Christ! Thus, unique prospects also include:

- Friends
- Neighbors
- Fellow Citizens

Shared Prospects

A second category that should be on every prospect list is *Shared Prospects*. Included in this category are:

➢ Church Visitors

➢ Contacts through Congregational Outreach

➢ Unknowns in the Community.

Concerning visitors to our assemblies, studies have cited that of our first time visitors 12-15% will become members; of second time visitors 40-45% will become members; and of third time visitors 60-75% will become members. We must reach our visitors.

A prompt response in contacting visitors also proves essential to church growth as those contacted within thirty-six hours have an 80% return rate; those contacted within seventy-two hours have a 60% return rate; while those contacted after seven days only have a 15% return rate. Some experts estimate that it takes seven contacts to reach potential visitors.

Informal "Info Cards" should be handed out and received the day of their first visit. Our "info cards" should ask similar questions to these:

• Do you have a church home?

• How familiar are you with the churches of Christ?

• Do you have any questions about anything you have seen in our worship?

Space for their address and phone number should be available. When these cards are filled out and received, a door will be opened for Bible study and/or a personal visit.

Christian visitors should meet with the elders of the congregation at some point before being allowed to place membership with the congregation. As overseers and protectors of the flock, such a meeting is the responsibility of elders.

Information gained from visitor cards will help the soul winner to have some information to engage in conversations and build a relationship with the visitor that hopefully would blossom into a friendship. Moreover, upon setting an appointment for Bible study, this information could be used to have casual conversations before each study begins. Such conversations could prove helpful in lowering any defenses or nervous tensions on either our part or the person we have invited for the study.

Concerning those touched through congregational outreach, there must *first* be congregational outreach in order for a list to be started. How can a congregation grow if they refuse to reach out? During such efforts as gospel meetings, Vacation Bible Schools, clothing giveaways, etc., someone(s) should be assigned the task of taking names, numbers, addresses, and interests for they sake of future conversations.

For benevolent efforts an informal "Info Card" would again be appropriate with similar questions. As these cards are collected, they should be marked according to interest. The names gathered should be formed into a prospect list and follow-up visits/calls assigned. As the list is formed, the names can be categorized by their interest and location of their homes. Different groups can do the follow-up according to the various communities. Bus routes then could be assigned for those needing transportation. New works could be implemented within the congregation to fill the growing need and members could be given new opportunities to work.

Concerning unknowns in the community, our outreach efforts give us a reason to make ourselves known to the unknowns. Never take for granted that people in the community know about the church, including the location of the meeting house.

Flyers and homemade doorknockers can be handed out for these occasions. Allow the children to take part in making the doorknockers. Get the entire congregation excited by knowing why you are having this campaign.

It would be a mistake to give the impression that you are planning to baptize 3,000 that day. Make clear that such efforts are merely introductory. A congregation can be discouraged if they are misled about why they are going out into the community.

We should understand such efforts are achieving the purpose of making ourselves known in the community and helping us to find those who might be interested in future studies. Follow up on those who expressed interest and/or attended by making an immediate appointment for a Bible study.

Radio, newspaper, television, door knocking, and mass mailings can help to advertise the church and promote awareness in the community. Such efforts should be considered as good ways of plowing the ground and preparing the soil.

However, these things should not be considered the end of our efforts, but as a means to having more Bible studies. It is not until we are having Bible studies with the lost that we are truly and effectively sowing the seed.

How a Prospect List Can Help Us to Bring More Souls to Jesus

A prospect list will help us to identify those in need. We should categorize each person according to their interest in studying (A: Most Interested; B: Some Interest; C: Little – No Interest).

We may have to work a while with some of our prospects to develop their interest before they are ready to be approached for a study. Upon a careful critique of their reactions, we can begin placing them according to the level of interest we believe they have shown and would have for a Bible study. The reason why we categorize prospects is to spend as much time studying with the "A" and "B" prospects as possible.

We should not completely ignore the "C" prospects. When given the opportunity, we should try to encourage every soul. From time to time we may want to write a card to our "C" prospects to let them know we are thinking about them. We should consider our time and enthusiasm to be precious. "C" prospects are thus categorized because they have little to no interest in anything religious. We must be careful not to lose our time and enthusiasm by approaching only "C" prospects. Why should we spend the majority of our few precious moments dealing with persons who have no real interest when there are others we know who are ready to receive the word? Would we not be more effective in winning souls by using our opportunities wisely?

Working from a prospect list will help us keep our responsibility to the lost ever before us. If we could have ten studies with "A" prospects in a year, it is reasonable to believe we could convert at least seven or eight of them using a proven method of Bible study.

If we have ten members in our congregation using the same approach with the same proven method, our congregation should see at least seventy to eighty baptisms per year. When a congregation will work together with a proven game plan, increase will come.

In Conclusion

Hopefully, a prospect list will keep pressed upon our hearts and consciences the responsibility we each have to commit the things we have seen and heard to others (2 Timothy 2:2). Do not make such a list only to put it aside.

Each one of us can be a soul winner for Jesus. Why not sit down and begin forming a prospect list today? Are we not "debtors" to these lost souls to give them at least the opportunity of hearing the gospel (Romans 1:14-16)?

"I looked on my right hand, and beheld, but there was no man that would know me: refuge failed me; no man cared for my soul" (Psalm 142:4).

Discussion Questions for Chapter Eighteen

Class Assignment: Each participant should begin working on a prospect list and discuss other possible prospects with the class, elders, or other soul winners.

19

Your Move

(Approaching a Soul for Christ)

Christ has commanded us to make disciples (Matthew 28:19). To make disciples of our prospects, we first must approach our prospects. Learning how to approach a prospect is essential to obeying the Great Commission.

Since the church grows through teaching and teaching depends upon our approach, can the church grow properly if we fail to approach our prospects? Let us not overcomplicate the matter, but strive to keep our approach as BASIC as possible.

Biblically Correct

We do not need to attempt to approach anyone if we are not going to speak the truth. Jesus did not approach the Samaritan woman with political correctness, but biblical correctness (John 4:4-26).

In those days, Jewish men did not speak to women in public the way Jesus did. Neither did Jews have dealings with Samaritans. But our Savior was not concerned with the political tide of His day; He was concerned with saving her soul.

Determining to be biblically correct in all that we teach is the *first* priority in approaching any prospect. Let's say we are going to approach a person who is living in adultery, or is continuing in some other form of willful sin. We must be determined to teach the truth on the subject before we ever approach that person. The teaching may not occur on our first visit with them, but at some point it must occur. The hope must remain that this person will repent and obey the gospel.

If we approach this prospect with the mindset that "we all sin" and "I am not their judge" we will most likely keep ourselves from teaching what needs to be taught most. Jesus certainly did not have this attitude, neither did His apostles. When Jesus spoke to the woman at the well about her "husband," He knew she was not married, but was instead living with a man. He did not bury the issue or act like it did not exist. He confronted the issue in an effort to help the woman repent. We must do the same in our efforts to save souls.

Attentive to the Prospect

When the prospect speaks, we must listen. Philip never would have been able to teach the eunuch had he not listened to the eunuch's question (Acts 8:30 ff.).

Philip had the right mindset; he was going to preach Jesus. But for this to happen, he had to approach the prospect and listen to the prospect.

Philip could have traveled all the way to Ethiopia with the eunuch and never baptized him had he not been listening to his concerns. Philip was attentive to the unique needs of the eunuch and it resulted in his conversion to Christ.

Our task is not to bombard our prospects with argumentation. We should not desire to place them on the "horns of a dilemma." As we have already discussed, a personal study is not a debate. The mindset for a debate and for a one-on-one study is completely different. In a debate, our concern is defending the truth. In a personal study, our concern is *sharing* the truth. However, in both cases, one had better listen to what the other is saying.

In debate we are dealing with people who have hardened their hearts to the truth. In personal studies we will most likely be teaching our friends and loved ones. Now, more than ever before, they are going to need us to be a friend and loved one by helping them to see the True Light.

Sincere in Attitude

The difference between a Christ-like approach and the approach made by religious con men is that we are not trying to "con" anyone. Our task requires no manipulating, forcing, or deceiving. Such con men are nothing more than "false apostles, deceitful workers, transforming themselves into the apostles of Christ" (2 Corinthians 11:13).

Our approach should reflect our cause. Our cause is truth, as it is in Jesus; and our approach should be one of complete honesty and truthfulness. What we hope to accomplish is a simple and sincere approach to a dear soul in need of salvation.

We are seeking to ask them about their unique spiritual needs, while hoping to provide them with the necessary help they need from God's word. "For we are not as many, which corrupt the word of God: but as of sincerity, but as of God, in the sight of God speak we in Christ" (2 Corinthians 2:17).

No one should be able to question our love and sincerity. Our devotion to the Lord and to the salvation of lost souls should be evident and unquestionable. We may not always go about it the right way. We may not always have the results we desire. But, we should not be blamed for lack of effort and for lack of caring.

Inviting in Our Approach

As Philip said to the Lord, the world is saying to us, "Show us the Father." Our intention is to show the Father through His word and demonstrate Him through our lives.

Our approach should be one which welcomes a person to know more about the God they seek. We are not seeking to threaten anyone, but to help them to learn.

Allow me to offer a couple of suggestions for you to use in your invitation to lost souls.

Invite a Person for a Bible Study.

Too many times we may be approaching people with the wrong invitation. Our invitation is usually an invitation to the services of the church. Why not first invite a person to Bible study, and upon some study, then invite that person to a worship service?

Foreign missionaries are tremendously successful because they use correspondence courses to develop interest. They will door-knock communities and enroll people in their correspondence courses. They will have others to help grade these courses. And, usually others will follow-up on these studies after a certain number have been completed. Only after a series of correspondence courses are completed will a follow-up be made and an invitation to attend the church's services extended.

Outside of curiosity, why would a person visit a worship service without first being convinced of the need to worship God? Granted, some knowledge and comfort gained from a worship service can do much to encourage a Bible study, but never should we leave our invitation at merely, "Do you want to come to church with me?"

Such an invitation leaves too great an opportunity to be declined. Sooner or later, a Bible study must take place with the lost soul – whether we or someone else will conduct it. Our goal is to approach a prospect with the hope of setting a Bible study appointment. If the prospect never looks into the Bible for his own sake, he can never be saved.

We should share with the prospect the benefits they will gain by accepting our invitation to study. Before we make the approach, we should have in mind the method of study we intend to use (VHS/DVD study series, correspondence courses, etc.).

The benefit of using correspondence courses is that such a method involves many others in the work. Soul winning becomes a team effort through this method.

The use of correspondence courses is not without its deterrents, however. A congregation's use of correspondence courses should not deter us from our personal responsibility as soul winners. Each member should continue attempting to reach the souls on their respective prospect lists. They should attempt to enroll these people in these correspondence courses, rather than forgoing their prospect lists.

Take Something with You.

A second recommendation I will offer for your visiting is this: take something with you. If you are going "cold" door-knocking, take tracts, correspondence courses, or your favorite one-to-one Bible studies.

If you are going to visit a friend, relative, or neighbor you know, take some jelly, homemade bread, etc., along with your literature. After you have visited for a minute, tell them about what your church is doing and offer the material to them. The ice will be broken, and it will be hard for them to be upset at your invitation to study the Bible over the smell of warm bread or pie!

Close the Deal

We must close the deal. After approaching the soul with a sincere attitude and biblically correct agenda, we are now ready to enroll them in correspondence courses or establish a day, time and place to begin a one-to-one Bible study – the sooner the better. As stated, have a series of studies in mind and, as the first study closes, make plans for a second. Even correspondence courses will require one-to-one studies to occur at some point.

To close the deal for a study, *both* the one approaching and the one being approached must be willing. A successful approach does not always end with a fixed study appointment. A person may remember your approach and contact you at a much later time. Continue to encourage that person, and continue to let them know you care.

In Conclusion

If we keep our approach as BASIC as possible, we should see a notable increase in the Bible study appointments we are able to set. The more studies we have, the more souls we will win for Christ.

As a result of such Bible studies, we will come to see dear souls change from being our prospects to our "joy in the Lord." Paul once wrote, "For what is our hope, or joy, or crown of rejoicing? Are not even ye in the presence of our Lord Jesus Christ at his coming? For ye are our glory and joy" (2 Thessalonians 2:19-20).

The beloved apostle was taking great joy in the thought and hope of forever being united with his dear friends and brethren in the Lord which he had helped to convert. All Christians should aspire to know such joy.

This joy is known only by faithful Christians who have dedicated themselves to the task of approaching the lost within their reach and sharing with them the gospel of truth. Do we have this joy in our salvation? Do we have this hope in the day of Christ?

"Seek ye the Lord while he may be found, call ye upon him while he is near: Let the wicked forsake his way, and the unrighteous man his thoughts: and let him return unto the Lord, and he will have mercy upon him; and to our God, for he will abundantly pardon" (Isaiah 55:6-7).

Discussion Questions for Chapter Nineteen

1.) Discuss why being biblically correct must be our foremost concern.

2.) Do you and/or your congregation have a Bible study method already in place? Discuss its benefits and possible improvements you would make if any.

3.) Develop a plan that will work for you and for your group to work together. You will need correspondence courses and/or Bible studies, volunteers to knock doors, volunteers to grade the courses, and volunteers to follow-up with those enrolled.

4.) Discuss ways in which you can include your prospect list in this effort. How would you use the material with your prospects?

20

The Great Commission

Over the next two chapters we will be addressing the command of the Great Commission to make disciples. The reason why we are dedicating two chapters to this study is first, because of the importance of the subject; and secondly, to provide a clearer understanding of what must be done.

The Great Commission serves a two-fold purpose. First, in His final commission, the Lord instructs His disciples on the subject of preaching and teaching so that they might be able to convert the lost and make disciples of them. When we study the Great Commission, we study the Savior's command and strategy for the conversion of every creature in all nations.

The second purpose of this commission is for the benefit of those who are outside of Christ. If the lost will hear and study the Great Commission, they will learn what they must do to be saved. As this commission instructs the church on those things which we are to teach, it necessarily instructs the lost on those things they should hear and receive to become converted disciples.

Our brief study of the church's marching orders will center upon this two-fold purpose. We wish to learn the exact nature of the commands which we are to teach, even the order of this commission, therefore learning the exact commands the lost must hear and obey to be made disciples.

Matthew 28:16-20 (NKJV)

"Then the eleven disciples went away into Galilee, to the mountain which Jesus had appointed for them. And when they saw Him, they worshiped Him; but some doubted. Then Jesus came and spoke to them, saying, 'All authority has been given to Me in heaven and on earth. Go therefore and make disciples of all the nations, baptizing them in the name of the Father and of the Son and of the Holy Spirit, teaching them to observe all things that I have commanded you; and lo, I am with you always, even to the end of the age.' Amen."

The Great Commission Is Perpetual

The first matter of controversy which we wish to address is pertaining to the perpetual nature of this command. From time to time someone will say that this passage applied only to the eleven disciples which were with the Lord. We can reject this teaching for the following reasons:

➢ Mathias and Paul would be excluded from the Great Commission if this teaching were true as neither one was there at that time;

➢ Paul instructed Timothy to teach faithful men so that they could teach others (2 Timothy 2:2).

➢ The apostles remained in Jerusalem while dispersed Christians carried the gospel into Samaria and the uttermost parts of the world (Acts 8:1-4) – a command initially spoken only to the eleven (Acts 1:2, 8). If this command spoken initially to the eleven could be carried out by others then, it can be carried out by others now.

➤ This commission is for Christians of every generation until our Lord returns.

Let us now turn our attention to the primary matter of our study which is making disciples of all nations (Matthew 28:19).

Making Disciples

Matthew 28:16-20, specifically vv.18-20, has been cited as the basis for our study. We have listed the passage as it has been translated in the New King James Version. However, we also shall be noting how other versions have translated this passage.

For example, the Authorized Version or King James Version translates *matheteusate* as "teach" rather than "make disciples." While teaching is certainly involved in disciple making, it would appear on the surface to be too narrow a definition.

In Alexander Campbell's *Living Oracles*, *matheteusate* is translated "convert." On the surface, this also seems to be too narrow a definition. However, in Campbell's mind, the idea of a conversion was anything but narrow.

Of conversion, Campbell wrote: "The entire change effected in man by the Christian system, consists in four things: a change of views; a change of affections; a change of state; and a change of life."[1]

Each change noted by Campbell should be considered carefully and proven by sacred Scripture rather than accepted on the basis of being *his* conclusion. However, when we turn to the Scriptures we find that each of these changes is certainly founded upon biblical teaching (see 1 Peter 2:9; Philippians 4:8; Ephesians 2:13; 2 Corinthians 5:16-21).

Having considered this, Campbell's translation of *matheteusate* is more accurate and deeper than we would first suppose.

To keep the Savior's command and *matheteusate* all nations, we must teach those things which would induce lost souls to be converted, thus becoming disciples.

W. Robertson Nicoll understood baptism as the sole "condition of discipleship" according to this passage in Matthew.[2] We have brethren who appear to be teaching the same thing today, and this is why we want to take the time to discuss this issue now.

A number of years ago I took issue with the idea that as long as a person is baptized for the remission of sins, that person is to be considered a brother in Christ. The question I raised was "What about the Mormons?" They baptize for the remission of sins, are we to consider Mormons as being Christians without being converted from their false ways?

---

[1] Alexander Campbell. *The Christian System* (Nashville, TN: Gospel Advocate Company, 2001), p. 44.
[2] W. Robertson Nicoll. *The Expositor's Greek New Testament*, vol. 1 (Grand Rapids, MI: Eerdmans Printing Company, 1974), p.339.

As I studied this question more, I came to realize that each person needs to be taught on an individual basis. If a person needs more help than others to understand the nature of true Christianity or the church, then we need to teach them. If they need to study why adultery is sinful and repent, then we must be willing to teach them.

To say that baptism is all that is required is to say that baptism is all that needs to be taught – and this could not be more wrong. Baptism is not the only condition for discipleship. While baptism is the culminating act that puts one into Christ and His covenant (Romans 6:3-7; Galatians 3:26-27), apart from belief and repentance, it is empty and vain. Man must obey this doctrine from the heart (Romans 6:17).

One must know the Lord in order to be a disciple. Jeremiah prophesied in the long ago that knowing the Lord would be a condition of entering the new covenant (Jeremiah 31:34); and the writer of Hebrews says the same (Hebrews 8:11). One cannot be a disciple of this covenant without first knowing the Lord.

Who Is a Disciple?

Jesus referred to His disciples as being "scribe(s) instructed concerning the kingdom of heaven" (Matthew 13:52).

Jesus also said, "A disciple is not above his teacher, but everyone who is perfectly trained will be like his teacher" (Luke 6:40).

A disciple is much more than a learner. A disciple is an attached follower. One can cease to be a disciple by ceasing to follow Jesus (John 6:66), thus "severing" themselves from Jesus (Galatians 5:4; NASB), thus becoming "estranged" from Christ (ibid; NKJV).

From scripture, we learn how the first disciples would come to set the right example of discipleship as they would eventually forsake all to sit at the feet of their Master (Luke 5:11). Decisions like this are not made without some comprehensive understanding of the decision being made.

Truly, a conversion – a change of view, affection, state and life – is being accomplished. It is no small thing to be made a disciple. And while it would be unreasonable to think that spiritually new born babes should have the same measure of understanding as that of disciples who have been learning for considerable amounts of time, we should not be so misguided to believe that only a shallow depth of spiritual understanding is essential.

Our teaching must offer the comprehensive understanding needed for a soul to make such changes as are required and become motivated to attach themselves to Jesus as His followers.

To say that baptism is the sole requirement would negate the command to believe as it is recorded by Mark (16:16). Also, Luke's account of the Great Commission, believed by some to be given after that of Matthew and Mark, emphasizes repentance, remission of sins, Christ and His kingdom, all to be preached in His name beginning at Jerusalem (Luke 24:46-49; Acts 2:1-11). If such sacred truths are to be taught, they must be heard and received as well.

The Order of the Great Commission

The idea of the Great Commission being taught as a series of commands is not uncommon to the churches of Christ. J.W. McGarvey believed the order followed accordingly:

"Having made disciples by persuading men to accept the teaching of Jesus, and having baptized such into the name of the Father and of the Son and of the Holy Spirit, they were next to teach them all that Jesus had commanded – all the duties of the Christian life."[3]

The view expressed by McGarvey is held among recent writers as well. Homer Hailey writes:

"The order Jesus gave was: make disciples by evangelizing, i.e., preaching the gospel to the lost, baptize, teach the baptized to observe all that He had commanded the apostles."[4]

It seems that both McGarvey and Hailey leave the door open for someone to make a case for discipleship before and without baptism. This is not to say that these men believed this to be the case, for they did not, but it does show some inconsistency in the view of the Great Commission being a series of commands.

Jack Cottrell is perhaps a little clearer and in better harmony with other scriptures as he writes:

---

[3] J.W. McGarvey. *A Commentary on Matthew and Mark* (Delight, AR: Gospel Light Publishing Company, n.d.), p254.

[4] Homer Hailey. *Carrying Out the Great Commission* (Louisville, KY: Religious Supply, Inc., n.d.), p.6.

"In terms of the Great Commission in Matthew 28:19-20, baptism is something taught *before* conversion with a view to *becoming* a disciple, while 'teaching them to observe all that I command you' *follows* conversion and deals with the details of the Christian life."[5]

While Cottrell appears to be clearer in preserving baptism as a condition of discipleship than was McGarvey or Hailey, he has not made a definitive statement on the matter. To say that teaching the converted to observe all things He has commanded *after* conversion is illogical at best and still leaves one with the impression that the commission is a series of commands.

Certainly, a great deal of teaching – if not most – remains to be comprehended after conversion; but how shall the lost be converted without observing any of the commandments of Christ? This view is also inconsistent, as we will elaborate momentarily, but do note that McGarvey did understand disciples as "having" been baptized.

To find a definitive statement on this matter, we turn to the prolific and lamented writer, T. Pierce Brown.

"It is my present judgment that there is ONE COMMAND in that commission, and the other parts of it are words or phrases telling how that command is to be obeyed."[6]

Brown continues by showing that "Go" is not an imperative, but is from the Greek word *poreuthentes*, which is a first

---

[5] Jack Cottrell. *Baptism a Biblical Study* (Joplin, MO: College Press, 2002), p.16.
[6] T. Pierce Brown. *Pertinent Principles* (vol.2), (Pulaski, TN: Sain Publications n.d.), p.144.

person aorist passive participle in the masculine plural, meaning "When you go, or wherever you go." Literally, "As you go, make disciples."

Thus, whatever we find ourselves doing in life, whether we are bricklayers or stay-at-home mothers, we must have the heart to carry out the Great Commission – that is, to make disciples. As we go, we must be teaching the lost and converting the lost in such a way that they are compelled to forsake all and follow Jesus.

The Great Commission is not a series of commands; it is one command. We are to make disciples. The Great Commission is a lifelong command. Christians must remain resolved to make disciples throughout the course of their new life in Christ.

How Do We Make Disciples?

Seeing that the first "step" in this so-called series of commands is not really a step at all, and that the "series" is not really a series of commands but one command, how shall we obey this command?

Our Lord has said, "As you go into the world, make disciples of all nations, baptizing them into the name of the Father and of the Son and of the Holy Spirit, teaching them to observe all things I have commanded you."

An everyday equivalent of this command would be a parent telling a child, "As you go into the swimming pool, swim, using your arms and legs, doing all the things which I have instructed you."

The command is to swim. The child could not swim without using his arms and legs. The Christian cannot make disciples without baptizing the lost. The child could not swim without doing all the parent had instructed *pertaining to swimming*.

Should we think the parent was talking about anything or everything outside of swimming? Why should we think the Lord was talking about anything or everything outside of making disciples?

In the context of Matthew 28:19-20, we have two present tense active participles: *baptizontes* which should always be translated "baptizing" and secondly, *didazkontes* which should always be translated "teaching."

One cannot be a disciple without first being taught. The command is to make disciples *having baptized* them and *having taught* them to observe all that He has commanded *pertaining to becoming a disciple*.

Unfortunately, some will object to this plainly stated command, wishing to hold to the idea of a series of commands, and argue it is impossible to teach all the Savior has commanded before baptism. Such an argument would be like saying it is impossible to teach a child all there is about swimming before throwing him into the pool!

If we allow the context to be the final determining authority for the meaning of this phrase, we can come to see that we are to teach all things He has commanded as these commands pertain to making disciples of all nations. It has been *assumed* that this phrase is speaking of the continued teaching necessary in the realm of Christian living, and such teaching is necessary, but this passage reveals only Christ's instructions on how to make and become disciples.

We must teach *all* that Christ has commanded in His plan of salvation. Some erroneously view the teaching which precedes baptism to be mere surface teaching and attempt to minimize the things a lost soul should know in order to be converted. Some are even turning a blind eye to sin and baptizing without penitence on the part of the believer. Some wish to limit *all things* to *some things* – specifically, baptism and the remission of sins.

Are we to conclude as did Nicoll, that baptism is the sole condition for discipleship? Accordingly, all one would have to be taught is that baptism is for the forgiveness of sins and they can become a disciple.

However, being a disciple involves much more than knowing that baptism is involved in the plan of salvation. We wish not to exclude the importance of baptism – by any means – but neither do we wish only to make disciples solely unto the doctrine of baptism. We are commanded to make disciples for Christ by teaching all relative commandments – not one specific teaching.

Certainly one cannot be a disciple without being baptized. Baptism holds its place as being part of the Great Commission. Matthew placed an emphasis on baptism as do many New Testament writers; but we must understand that hearing the gospel (Mark 16:15), believing the gospel message (Mark 16:16), and repenting of sins (Luke 24:47) holds equal importance in the Great Commission even though these are not as strongly emphasized by Matthew. Possibly, a case can be made for confession of Christ in the act of being baptized into His name as we are baptized into the names of the Sacred Three (Matthew 28:19; Acts 2:38).

For us to learn what we must teach to make disciples we must ask, what did the apostles and early evangelists teach in order to make disciples?

➢ Did they not preach faith (Acts 16:31)?

➢ Did they not teach repentance (Acts 17:30-31)?

➢ Did they not teach the kingdom (Acts 8:12; Acts 19:8; Acts 20:25; Acts 28:23, 31)?

➢ Did they not preach baptism upon the basis of belief, repentance, and confession (Acts 22:16)?

➢ In short, they preached Jesus (Acts 8:35).

➢ They preached all the things that He had commanded pertaining to becoming a disciple.

➢ They preached to convert the lost to Christ.

One could do as Owen Olbricht has done and make a list of everything taught by the apostles and early evangelists in order to convert lost souls. His efforts led to the compilation of a list of at least eight things which a person ought to know before being baptized.[7]

1.) There is one true God (Acts 3:13; 14:15; 17:23-31).

---

[7] Owen Olbricht. *Baptism: A Response of Faith* (Delight, AR: Gospel Light Publishing Company, 2000), pp.56-57.

2.) Jesus is Lord and Christ, the Son of God (John 20:30-31; Acts 2:36; 4:10; 5:42; 9:20, 22; 10:36; 17:3; 18:5, 28).

3.) The word of the Lord saves (Acts 11:14; 16:32; 2 Timothy 4:2).

4.) Jesus is the Savior (Acts 2:32; 8:5, 25, 35; 14:7, 21; 16:10; 1 Corinthians 2:1, 2; 15:1-4).

5.) Without Jesus we are lost and in need of forgiveness (Acts 4:10-12).

6.) We need to repent, that is, to change our lives (Acts 2:38; 3:19; 17:30).

7.) Sins are forgiven when we are baptized (Acts 2:38; 22:16).

8.) The truth concerning the kingdom of God was preached (Acts 8:12; 19:8; 20:25; 28:23, 31).

In Conclusion

We must be sure to convert people to Christ. If we are not careful we can find ourselves studying with the lost in order to convert them to baptism. Once they have come to accept baptism for remission of sins we can mistakenly feel that our mission is accomplished.

However, being converted to Christ requires more than just understanding what the Bible teaches about baptism. If baptism is the primary purpose of our study with lost souls, something is lacking. Such a study needs a "cross" in it!

Moreover, we can find ourselves extending fellowship to others solely on the basis of baptism for the remission of sins. If we are going to do that, why not just throw the rest of the Bible away?

If we will do as Christ has commanded and prove to be soul winners by teaching the entirety of His plan of salvation, we have the promise that He will be with us always, "even until the end of the world" (KJV).

Let us put our faith in Him who will never leave us nor forsake us (Hebrews 13:5), lest we forget the souls who depend upon us to teach them the whole counsel of God and the account we someday shall give.

"Yet if thou warn the wicked, and he turn not from his wickedness, nor from his wicked way, he shall die in his iniquity; but thou hast delivered thy soul. Again, When a righteous man doth turn from his righteousness, and commit iniquity, and I lay a stumblingblock before him, he shall die: because thou hast not given him warning, he shall die in his sin, and his righteousness which he hath done shall not be remembered; but his blood will I require at thine hand. Nevertheless if thou warn the righteous man, that the righteous sin not, and he doth not sin, he shall surely live, because he is warned; also thou hast delivered thy soul" (Ezekiel 3:19-21).

Discussion Questions for Chapter Twenty

1.) How many commandments are found in the Great Commission?

2.) Who is a disciple?

3.) How do we make disciples?

4.) Discuss the difference in converting a person to baptism and converting a person to Christ.

21
Making Disciples

In this chapter we will be continuing our thoughts from the previous chapter pertaining to the Great Commission. Jesus gave the church marching orders when He commanded, "Go therefore and make disciples of all nations" (Matthew 28:19, NKJV).

The point we have stressed is that we must be found converting people to Christ and His kingdom, rather than to the doctrine of baptism for the remission of sins. Make no mistake, in order to be converted one must be baptized for the remission of sins (cf. Acts 2:38; Acts 22:16); but our studies and efforts to convert the lost must not be solely about baptism.

Let me share with you an experience I had as a very young preacher. I had a study with a man, his wife, and his brother. I was blessed to baptize all three that day. They attended one or two services and then went back to the Baptist Church. I failed to convert them to true New Testament Christianity. Now, I convinced them of the need to be baptized for the remission of sins; but I failed to teach adequately "all things" Christ commanded in order to become disciples of His.

Allow me to share with you a reoccurring experience I have in personal studies and conversations with people. It is not uncommon to speak with people who were baptized into a denomination about baptism for the remission of sins and to have them say, "I was baptized for the remission of sins." I will ask them if they said a sinner's prayer before baptism and the will usually acknowledge that they did. Then I will have to educate them as to what that particular denomination teaches and what the Bible teaches one must do to be saved.

Much time is usually spent on the subject of baptism in such cases, and it should be. However, the real problem is that these souls have spent years in manmade churches and they need to know about the church of the Bible. As faithful men have preached for years, "A person cannot be taught wrong and baptized right."

In an upcoming chapter we will dedicate it entirely to the study of converting one who was baptized into a denomination. The main point we wish to consider is the difference between the denominational plan of conversion and the gospel plan of salvation. For now, it is sufficient to say that we must make disciples for Christ and His kingdom. In order to do so we must teach all things pertaining to becoming a Christian.

Our present lesson will focus on four points which should never be overlooked by Christians as they seek to teach all things He has commanded. We have selected these points as they appear to be the most often overlooked in the present generation. Let us discuss these points with an attitude of seeking to understand and wishing always to improve in the service we render in the Name most holy (Acts 4:12; Philippians 2:9).

God's Plan Involves Hearing
and Properly Receiving His Word

Every man – sinner and saint alike – must receive the word of God (Acts 8:14; James 1:21). It is a commandment that is both initial and perpetual. We can receive the word of God when we initially hear it and we must continue to receive the word of God throughout life.

To become a disciple, each person must hear and receive the word of God. Man is to receive the word of God "with meekness" (James 1:21); even as a "little child" (Mark 10:15; Luke 18:17); and "with all readiness of mind" (Acts 17:11).

To receive in this sense simply means to give ear to; to embrace; to accept; to approve; to welcome; to be open to; and even to make it one's own (see the following lexicons for further study: Thayer, BDAG, Abbot-Smith; see also *"dexo-mai"* and *"apodexomai"* in Kittel, *Theological Dictionary of the New Testament*, Vol. II, p.55).

"How shall they hear without a preacher?" We cannot make disciples if we do not share with sinful men God's plan to save. Pressure to teach others can be alleviated simply by keeping in mind that the power is not in us, but in the gospel (Romans 1:16).

God's word is sufficient to prick a person's heart. The gospel is all we need. Any attempt to modify the gospel would lead to the certain destruction of the prospect's soul as well as our own (1 Corinthians 9:16; Galatians 1:6-9; 2 Thessalonians 1:7-10).

237

When we teach nothing but the gospel, we offer a sweet savor unto God (2 Corinthians 2:14-17). Therefore, we must follow Paul's instructions to Timothy and, "Take heed unto thyself, and unto the doctrine; continue in them: for in doing this thou shalt both save thyself, and them that hear thee" (1Timothy 4:16).

We can become so overly zealous in hoping to satisfy a prospect that we will find ourselves speaking words the prospect *wants* to hear while neglecting the words the prospect *needs* to hear. If we have manipulated or deceived a person into being baptized by modifying the gospel, we have accomplished nothing. The gospel must be obeyed from the heart and from the Bible to free a person from their sins (Romans 6:17-18).

We can also be too zealous to the point of overwhelming a prospect with too much too soon. We should use a method of Bible study which enables us to teach the prospect at a pace which they feel comfortable enough to learn. The Bible should be studied reasonably, and point by point, rather than jumping around with no real point being discussed fully.

Lost souls must be given a legitimate opportunity to receive the word and judge on their own accord what they must do to be saved. Studying point by point (or theme by theme) at a comfortable pace will give prospects a true opportunity to learn and receive the word of God. One may also wish to develop trust by simply studying a book at a time. The book of Acts is ideal for such studies.

God's Plan Involves Repentance

A prospect must be convicted of sin. Conviction of sin usually does not occur when someone is being *told* of their sinful and lost condition. Such sorrow more often occurs when a person has learned from God's word *on their own accord* that his ways are erring.

Our work is to help the lost soul learn and accept the truth by his or her volition. If God's word is studied truthfully, sinners will be convicted of their sins. Our goal should be to help lost souls realize this righteous conviction. Godly sorrow leads to repentance (2 Corinthians 7:9). Repentance leads to salvation (Luke 13:3; Acts 3:19; 2 Corinthians 7:10). A sinner cannot be saved without repenting of sins (Luke 13:3-5; 2 Peter 3:9). We must repent of sins in order to be saved (Acts 8:20-23).

To illustrate repentance we have Paul's words to the idol worshippers of Lystra as he beckoned unto them to "turn from these vanities unto the living God" (Acts 14:15). Repentance is a turning; it is a change of direction. Whatever the sin may be, the sinner must turn from it, leave it behind, and begin serving God.

One cannot serve sin and God. He must turn from the vanities of sin unto the living God.

Seeing then the absolute necessity of repentance, why would we fail by neglecting to teach this concept to a lost and dying soul? Our job is unfulfilled if repentance has not been preached.

239

Moreover, as a Christian and as a congregation, we cannot extend fellowship to someone who is not in fellowship with God. 1 Corinthians 5 teaches us of such a situation wherein a brother had to repent. The church was not to act like his actions were acceptable. The church was to "put away the wicked one" until he repented. When he did repent, they were to forgive him in the spirit of Christ (cf. 2 Corinthians 2; 7).

God's Plan Involves One Baptism

One cannot fully receive or accept the word of God until he has obeyed its teaching and been baptized. We find that 3,000 souls "gladly received" the word on Pentecost "and were baptized" (Acts 2:41).

We learn that certain citizens of the city of Samaria "received the word of God" (Acts 8:14) when they accepted the "preaching of the kingdom" and "were baptized" (Acts 8:12).

Cornelius and his near friends and kinsmen "received the word of God" when they yielded in obedience to its teaching and were baptized (Acts 10:48).

The Bible teaches us of one baptism commanded by God for every sinner to obey (Ephesians 4:5). With the heart, man believes *unto* righteousness and with the mouth confession is made *unto* salvation (Romans 10:10). Man must repent and be converted (Acts 3:19). God granted the Gentiles repentance *unto* life (Acts 11:18). However, baptism is not an act which leads one *unto* Christ, but rather, baptism is the culminating point at which one is added or enters *into* Christ and

His spiritual body which is the church (Acts 2:41; Romans 6:3-4; Galatians 3:26-27).

When one is baptized scripturally he comes into a spiritual union with Christ and his life is brought into harmony with the will of God, being reconciled by the blood of Christ. We shall now note ten earmarks of the one baptism of the new covenant:

1.) The one baptism is a result of hearing the gospel preached (Mark 16:15; Acts 8:12; Acts 8:35; Romans 6:17).

2.) The one baptism is preceded by belief and repentance (Acts 2:38; Acts 3:19).

3.) The one baptism is in water (Acts 8:35-39; Ephesians 5:26).

4.) The one baptism is an immersion (Romans 6:3-4).

5.) The one baptism is in the name of (by authority and with approval) the Father, Son, and Holy Spirit (Matthew 28:19).

6.) The one baptism is for the forgiveness of our sins (Acts 2:38; Acts 22:16; Romans 6:3-7; Colossians 2:12-13).

7.) The one baptism is for our salvation (Mark 16:16; 1 Peter 3:21).

8.) The one baptism puts us into a covenant with Christ (Galatians 3:27).

9.) The one baptism is the point at which God adds one to His church (Acts 2:41, 47).

241

10.)The one baptism is to be practiced until the Lord comes again (Matthew 28:18-20).

If God's word is studied truthfully, and the message of the cross pricks the heart, the sinner will reach this conclusion and be convicted of the need to be baptized. The power is in the word!

God's Plan Involves Faithful Living

Are we striving to baptize *only* or are we striving to teach *all* the Lord has commanded? We must be careful not to view baptisms as notches on our pistols. Souls are more than notches!

We must not help lost souls to be baptized *only* and leave them to fend for themselves by not providing them with any means of encouragement and continued growth. Lost souls must be taught of the necessity to continue as followers of Jesus. After they are converted, they must continue to be taught the virtues of Christian living (see 2 Peter 1:5-11).

As soul winners we certainly need to teach the truth of baptism. But, we also need to teach lost souls about the duties and responsibilities awaiting them upon their decision to be converted. Otherwise, how can we say they are converted? Rather than saving such teaching for after the fact, we should help them to accept this truth before baptism.

The fallacy in saving such teaching for "another day" is oftentimes that day never comes. Furthermore, how can one be truly converted to Christ and His cause without such teaching?

Our work as personal evangelists is unfulfilled if the new Christian we have converted is never seen or heard from again. They should be encouraged to be a member of your home congregation and considered as family. They must know the life that awaits them in Christ is one of righteous living, self-sacrifice, and fellowship with God's people.

In Conclusion

We must first receive and obey the word of God if we are to help others to receive and obey the word. We must be faithful disciples in order to help make faithful disciples.

Let us faithfully determine to live righteously and help others to grow as we have grown in the grace and knowledge of the Lord (2 Peter 3:18). Every seed brings forth fruit after its kind. The fruit of faithful Christians will be faithful Christians.

"Another parable put he forth unto them, saying, The kingdom of heaven is like to a grain of mustard seed, which a man took, and sowed in his field: Which indeed is the least of all seeds: but when it is grown, it is the greatest among herbs, and becometh a tree, so that the birds of the air come and lodge in the branches thereof" (Matthew 13:31-32).

Discussion Questions for Chapter Twenty-One

1.) Why is it important that we teach lost souls more than simply the doctrine of baptism?

2.) Discuss the idea of receiving the word of God.

3.) Discuss repentance in God's plan.

4.) Discuss baptism in God's plan.

5.) Is the baptism of a person the ending of God's plan and our responsibilities as teachers?

22
Teaching a Member of a Denomination

When one studies the Bible, he will find denominational-ism to be a perplexing issue. To find the practice of denomi-nationalism, one cannot turn to the Scriptures. No denomina-tions are found in them. And, if no denominations can be found in the Bible, obviously no denominational baptisms will be found in the Bible. No apostle, prophet, or inspired teacher ever had to address this specific issue for his day and time. We must, therefore, learn from the Scriptures what the one baptism is so that we can know what it is not. We must then be determined to help these precious souls know and obey the truth. It is not a question of *if* a soul winner will face the issue of denominational baptism, but *when*.

Studies in Acts

Three times in Acts the question of what one must do to be saved was raised (Acts 2:37; Acts 9:6; Acts 16:30). Three times the answer was given according to the spiritual under-standing of the individual(s) asking.

Pentecost (Acts 2)

On Pentecost, believers were told to repent and be baptized in the name of Jesus for the forgiveness of their sins (Acts 2:38). These souls believed, were instructed to repent, and to

245

be baptized. The blessings they would receive were the forgiveness of sins, the gift of the Holy Spirit, and being added to the Lord's church.

On that day, 3,000 souls believed, repented of sins, and were baptized in the name of Christ (which also implies a confession of Christ as Lord). They heard the gospel preached, believed what they heard, repented of their sins, confessed Christ, and were baptized for the forgiveness of sins.

Saul of Tarsus (Acts 9, 22)

Saul saw a vision of Christ on the Damascus Road. He believed in Jesus while upon that road. He asked Jesus what he must do and Jesus told him to go to Damascus and wait to be told what he must do from there.

For three days in Damascus he prayed and fasted (proof of repentance) (Acts 9:9, 11). When Ananias came to him, he told Saul of God's plan for him, laid his hands on him so that he could receive his sight, and commanded him to arise and be baptized and wash away his sins calling on the name of the Lord (Acts 22:16).

If a three minute "sinner's prayer" could wash away sins *today*, why didn't a three day sinner's prayer wash away sins *then*?

Saul was a penitent believer who was commanded to be baptized so that he might be forgiven and become a child of God. Saul heard the gospel, believed the gospel, repented of his sins, confessed Christ, and was baptized to wash away his sins.

The Philippian Jailor (Acts 16)

The jailor had yet to believe in Jesus when he asked Paul and Silas what he needed to do to be saved. When he asked what he must do to be saved, he was told, "Believe on the Lord Jesus Christ, and thou shalt be saved, and thy house" (Acts 16:31).

He was not a believer when he asked, and thus he was told to believe. Paul and Silas proceeded to teach him and his household so that they might believe. For this man and those of his house to believe in Jesus, they first had to hear the gospel preached and obey it.

The jailor heard the gospel preached and then washed the stripes which had been beaten upon the backs of Paul and Silas (proof of repentance). Paul then took them the same hour of the night and baptized them according to the command of Christ (Acts 16:33; Mark 16:15-16). After being baptized, these new Christians, Paul, and Silas went back into the house, ate, and rejoiced together (Acts 16:34).

Paul in Ephesus (Acts 19)

Paul also took this approach when teaching twelve men in Ephesus who had been taught only the baptism of John the Baptist (Act 19). The question Paul asked in Ephesus should be asked today everywhere the word is taught – "Unto what then were ye baptized?" (Acts 19:3)

While John's baptism was also for the remission of sins (Mark 1:4), it was no longer valid after the crucifixion and resurrection of our Lord. Souls confessed their sins according to John's baptism (Mark 1:5), but they did not confess Christ as Lord. Accordingly, these men were taught the truth about Christ's baptism and His kingdom and were baptized in the name of the Lord (Acts 19:4-5).

Philip and the Eunuch (Acts 8)

Another example of such teaching is found in the eighth chapter of Acts. Philip taught the eunuch about Jesus. He began with what the eunuch understood and explained unto him what he did not understand. The eunuch reached the conclusion that he needed to be baptized (Acts 8:36). Upon his confession of Christ, he was immersed (Act 8:37-38).

Philip preached Christ to the eunuch just as he had done in Samaria (Acts 8:5), and this included "preaching things pertaining to the kingdom of God" (Acts 8:12). Just as one cannot preach Christ without preaching baptism, one cannot preach Christ without preaching the kingdom.

In each of the cases we have studied we find six things in common:

1.) The gospel was preached and heard.

2.) The gospel was believed.

3.) The person(s) repented of sin.

4.) The person(s) confessed Christ.

5.) Baptism (immersion) in water occurred for the forgiveness of sin.

6.) From the point of baptism onward, the person(s) lived for Christ.

Studies in Denominational Baptisms

A person's denominational baptism might mirror the baptism of the New Testament in some ways. Many denominations immerse in water, but they do so "because a person has been saved" in their minds, rather than in order to be saved. The reason for their baptism is different than the reason stipulated in the New Testament. Baptism is never called "an outward sign of an inward grace" in the Bible. Baptism is never a condition of denominational church membership either.

Yet, it remains clear: if we can take only the Bible and find that baptism is an immersion and agree with others who have done the same, we can also take only the Bible and learn why one must be baptized and have agreement as well.

Some denominations baptize for the remission of sins. Yet, many of these groups teach egregious error concerning the Holy Spirit, Christ, God, and the church. Remember, the twelve in Ephesus had been taught a baptism for the remission of sins, but they had not been taught the truth about Jesus. These men were taught correctly about Jesus and then were immersed into Christ for the remission of sins.

Every soul must first repent in order to be baptized scripturally (Acts 2:38; Acts 3:19). Seeing that many churches and preachers among us are neglecting such teaching, how can we be confident that a denomination has taught the truth on this essential subject?

Other denominations sprinkle and pour water instead of immersion. Many of these groups will do this to infants who have never sinned, believed, repented, or confessed. In such cases, we must show them that baptism is an immersion in water; baptism is for penitent believers; and baptism is for the forgiveness of sin.

In Conclusion

Paul said, "I am pure from the blood of all men. For I have not shunned to declare unto you all the counsel of God" (Acts 20:26-27).

The only way we can be pure or free from the blood of all men is to do as Paul and preach all the counsel of God. To compromise is to lose our soul and to leave a lost soul in error.

With each person who comes to us from a denomination, let us begin by seeking to understand what they know and where they are spiritually speaking. Beginning with their understanding, let us teach them the truth about Jesus and obedience to His gospel. By so doing, we too will be free from the blood of all men.

"There is one body, and one Spirit, even as ye are called in one hope of your calling; One Lord, one faith, one baptism, One God and Father of all, who is above all, and through all, and in you all" (Ephesians 4:4-6).

Discussion Questions for Chapter Twenty-Two

1.) What must be our attitude toward those baptized in denominations?

2.) What can we learn from cases of conversion in Acts?

3.) What do these accounts of conversion have in common?

4.) When someone comes to us from a denomination and has not done what the Bible teaches about baptism, what must we do?

23
Converting an Atheist

Christians are in the midst of a tremendous conflict of world views and we must prepare ourselves for battle and persevere until the fight is won. However, not all atheists are adversarial. Some simply do not know the truth and need to be taught. When seeking to teach an atheist, we must keep in mind that we are hoping to help save a soul.

To convert an atheist, we first must convince him of the errors of atheism. Nothing good has ever resulted from atheism. No good can ever come from atheism. It is a lie of the devil. The Bible says that it is a fool who says in his heart, "There is no God" (Psalm 53:1).

In the case of naturalists, whose "god" is the creation rather than the Creator (see Romans 1:18-32), they need to be convinced that their perception of reality is not the answer. Some have sought to approach this subject with deep, often scientific facts and theories. Seeing that this author is no scientist, and that most Christians and atheists do not understand the scientific jargon which surrounds typical Christian – Atheist debates, soul winners must see the need for common sense questions and language.

How would we teach that uncle who never went to college? How would we teach the hard working soul who has tremendous common sense, but not a lot of scholastic learning or experience? With sincere intentions and wishing to learn how to teach such ones, the following discussion is centered upon what we believe to be "people's arguments" rather than scientific rhetoric and data.

It is Either God or Rocks and Dirt

For every effect there must be a reasonable cause. The universe either exists due to a reasonable cause or it does not. The atheist believes the universe has no reasonable cause. In order to justify his beliefs, he must ignore the plain facts of nature.

Let us examine the principle of cause and effect. How was your house built? Was the house built by a carpenter and his crew? Or, was the house built by a spontaneous explosion at the hardware store?

Now then, ask yourself, "How was the universe created?" Was this vast universe created by a Creator (Isaiah 45:11-12)? Or, did it come to exist from a spontaneous explosion of rocks and dirt?

The atheist has no evidence, only a *necessary assumption*. If rocks and dirt did not create the universe, there must be a cause greater than rocks and dirt which did. Here are some possible questions to ask an atheist:

➢ Can you tell me what caused the first mass of rocks and dirt?

➢ Can you provide me with any evidence of lifeless rocks and dirt creating life today?

➤ Can you provide me with any evidence of lifeless rocks and dirt *ever* creating life?

➤ Can you provide me with another explanation for your existence other than your evolving from lifeless rocks and dirt?

The Universe Was Either Created with Design and Order or Out of Chaos and Chance

Design and order is clearly seen in our universe. For the atheist to justify his religion, he must ignore the marvelous and awesome design and order which governs all existence.

To help an atheist to see design and order through common sense, we offer these possible scenarios.

➤ Let's say we take a visit together to a museum. In the museum, you see a working replica of our solar system. Did this replica occur by chaos and chance *or* by design and order?

If the replica needs a creator, why should not the real thing?

➤ Let's say in the doctor's office you find models of the human skeletal system and human organs. Do you suppose these models evolved over millions of years?

If it is impossible for something non-living to evolve, how is it possible for something non-living to begin the evolutionary process?

Life Either Originated from Something (or Someone) Living or Life Originated from the Non-Living

We have evidence that life begets life (e.g. birth; seed bearing plants). We have no evidence of dead matter ever begetting life. Consider the following:

> Life is essential to the evolutionary process.

> But, no evidence exists of life now or ever evolving from lifeless rocks and dirt.

> Therefore, Atheists cannot prove by evidence that evolution ever has occurred.

How can atheism and evolution stand without any proof? Without proof, we are without reason to accept this doctrine.

Soul winners must keep the atheist thinking by asking questions his religion cannot answer – and make no mistake, atheism is a religion. Note the following questions along this line of reasoning:

> Can you provide *one* example of existing evidence proving a rock or some other form of dead matter has produced on its own accord a living thing?

> If you cannot provide one example of such evidence today, do you have *any proof* of this *ever* taking place?

> If you cannot provide any evidence of this occurring today and you do not have any evidence of this phenomenon ever occurring, why should any man believe this doctrine?

The atheist/humanist religion of evolution cannot prove:

> Dead rocks and dirt ever spontaneously exploded to cause the universe.

> Life evolved without first having life.

> Dead rocks and dirt have ever had (including now) creative and life-giving power.

Without being able to prove each of these points, let alone even one of them, the religion of atheism is as lifeless as it would have us to believe of God. Why choose atheism? No evidence exists to support this religion.

The only way one can know there is no life after death is to live after death! A living person cannot know assuredly that life does not exist after death, for he has yet to die. The only atheist that does know there is life after is the dead atheist – and these souls are atheists no longer!

The Bible is given so that we can study and know assuredly of life after death. Time and again it has proven itself to be the eternal word of God, and the Bible will read the same after death as it does today.

Staying with the same line of reasoning, the only way the atheist can know there is no God is to be God! The only way to know God did not create the earth is to have been there and created it yourself (cf. Job 38)!

O how foolish the atheist religion truly is! It cannot be proven. It provides no good thing, no endearing, enduring quality essential to the fabric of society, man's happiness, and peace on earth. It is a hopeless, sad religion which has its ending already pronounced in the word of God – they are without excuse (Romans 1:20).

The only reason one could give for atheism is an anti-God bias. We reiterate: atheism is not the answer.

Which Came First: The Human Baby or the Human Mother?

This simple question has been used very effectively by gospel preachers in debates against highly-educated atheists. It proves to be very effective still.

From this question, we can see for ourselves the simplicity, yet profoundness, of such common sense reasoning. No being of any kind has ever been transformed into a human being mid-life. No being other than a human being can ever give birth to another human being.

Atheism cannot explain which came first, but the Bible does (Genesis 2:18 ff.). The Bible explains that man was first formed by God from the dust of the earth and that God breathed into his nostrils and he became a living being. The Bible explains how woman was created. The Bible also explains that all flesh shall return to the dust from whence it came, but the spirit – the life essence of man – shall return to God who gave it (Ecclesiastes 12:7).

Why not pose this question to an atheist and see what kind of reply you receive?

What Is the Answer?

Why should a person choose the religion of Christ? Why should one believe there is a God in heaven and that He gave His only Son for our salvation? We must not only be prepared to ask questions, we must also be prepared to answer them.

All the evidence of creation points to God. By our common sense reasoning, we have proven:

➤ A Creator exists.

➤ A Creator has always existed.

➤ Our Creator is a living being.

➤ Our Creator is proven superior to man in intelligence and power by giving life, design and order to the universe.

Common sense tells us that a cause must exist – a first cause. We believe that first cause is the God of the Bible. We believe this to be true because of the Bible. Common sense will only take us so far. We also need divine revelation.

The Bible is God's revelation of His will and attributes to man. We believe the Bible is completely inspired. God is real, sovereign, ruling over heaven and earth. Jesus Christ is His only Son, born of a virgin, crucified for our sins, resurrected by the power of His Father, and received into heaven. The Bible tells us so.

Men wrote the Bible as God inspired them to write (2 Timothy 3:15-17). The earmarks of inspiration include:

(1) **Impartiality.** There is no attempt to conceal a hero's sins, no toning down, and no apology. A biblical hero's sins and the sins of Sodom and Gomorrah are equally told in the fullest detail.

(2) **Consistent Emotions.** Inspired writers remained just as calm when speaking of great miracles as when retelling normal daily activities.

(3) **Brevity.** How would an uninspired human know what to write, what should be included, and what should be omitted?

(4) **Infallibility.** These men spoke on subjects that have baffled the greatest thinkers in human history – e.g. deity, angels, spirits, creation, existence, death, eternity. Yet, on all subjects and on all occasions they spoke with a confidence which knew no hesitation, and which admits no possibility of mistake.

(5) **The Power to Convict Men of Sin and Reform Lives.** God, who knows all things, related a story to us that speaks to the spirit of man and sustains those who hunger and thirst after righteousness.

The characteristics we have been discussing can be accounted for only by the fact that inspired men were writing under the guidance and restraining power of the Holy Spirit. Scarcely could one of these attributes exist without God's inspiration, yet alone *all* of them.

The God of the Bible is not just the creator and sustainer of life, He is our Father. He loves, teaches, disciplines, and nurtures His children. All who are in Christ are His children (Galatians 3:26-27).

Jesus is Lord and Christ (Acts 2:36). Jesus is the Lamb of God (John 1:29), which was slain from the foundation of the world (1 Peter 1:19-20; Revelation 13:8). Not only was Christ with God at the beginning of the world, He was directly responsible for the things we see and know even to the extent that nothing was made that was not made by Him (John 1:3-4; Colossians 1:15).

Jesus is deity incarnate. He is of a divine nature. He is God (John 1:1-3).

In Conclusion

What shall be the story of our lives – faith or folly? Will we know victory or defeat? Will we live and die according to the religion revealed by God, or according to a religion which denies God?

Alexander Campbell once debated an atheist named Robert Owen. The two became friends. Once, while visiting Campbell at his home at Bethany, Owen said, "The difference between you and me is that you have fear in death, while I do not." Campbell pondered this statement for a moment and then replied, "That is true. I have fear in death. But I also have hope." He then pointed to an ox and said, "You are like that brut over there; for he neither has fear or hope in death."

To live obediently as a faithful Christian is to have hope in death. May such studies as these help the soul winning Christian to be confident in the faith once delivered and contend for it earnestly (Jude 3). God exists and He is the rewarder of all who seek Him diligently (Hebrews 11:6). Let us tell it today!

"The heavens declare the glory of God; and the firmament sheweth his handywork" (Psalm 19:1).

Discussion Questions for Chapter Twenty-Three

1.) Is evolution established upon proven scientific experiments and evidence? If not facts, upon what is the atheist religion established?

2.) Upon what facts is the Christian religion based?

3.) Discuss the importance in our understanding the inspiration of the Bible.

4.) Discuss any other "common sense" questions you can offer to an atheist.

24
Restoring the Erring

"Brethren, if a man be overtaken in a fault, ye which are spiritual, restore such an one in the spirit of meekness; considering thyself, lest thou also be tempted. Bear ye one another's burdens, and so fulfill the law of Christ" (Galatians 6:1-2).

Have you ever heard a Christian say, "If we just could get our wayward members back in the church, we would have a much larger congregation."

Christians in congregations throughout this land echo a similar lament. Restoring the erring is a biblically legitimate concern to those who are worried for their brother's soul and long to see the church grow.

Before Christians can restore the erring as the Bible instructs, we must know who the erring are and why the Lord considers them to be in error.

A wayward member is usually identified as someone who has not been attending church services (cf. Hebrews 10:25-26). However, their lack of participation is usually a surface issue indicative of a much deeper problem. We might call it the "tip of the iceberg."

Numerous studies have been done to help us understand why people leave the church. Possible explanations include:

➢ The wayward was never grounded in the faith.

265

- The wayward was never truly converted.

- The wayward would rather be doing something recreational on Sundays.

- Work took the wayward away from the church.

- A spouse took the wayward away from the church.

- The wayward became upset at something or someone in the church.

- The wayward coveted some sin or sinful activity more than a relationship with the church. Rather, than repent, the wayward quit the church so as not to be a "hypocrite."

- The wayward moved to a new area and never identified with a congregation in that place.

- The wayward "just quit going."

Having identified some of the reasons a person becomes wayward, let us seek to understand what is required in order for such a one to be restored.

What Is a "Restoration"?

Public responses are generally categorized as baptisms and restorations. However, not every response categorized as a "restoration" is a restoration.

Faithful members may come forward asking for prayers for any number of reasons. They could be sick or soon to have surgery. They could be having a personal trial and/or struggle with sin and wish to solicit prayers for strength and increased faithfulness.

Such instances do not signify an unfaithful Christian coming forward for restoration, but a faithful Christian coming forward because they walk faithfully in His light (see 1 John 1:7-9).

To restore a Christian is to put that brother or sister "in the order of their former condition," even "to make them what they ought to be."

In the Parable of the Prodigal Son, the Lord illustrated to perfection the idea of a restoration. The son separated himself from his father. He was not where he should have been. He was wayward.

The son then proceeded to squander his inheritance on immoral living. After he had wasted his inheritance, he began to be in want and need. He found himself to be without an inheritance, without friends, and longing to eat the swill which he had fed to the hogs. His condition was not what it should have been.

The prodigal son needed to be restored to his father's house, his former manner of living, and his former condition. When Christians prove to be in this condition, they too need to be restored.

Who Restores an Erring Brother?

An erring Christian is restored ultimately by God. God forgives and restores the erring child's inheritance to what it once was. The father of the prodigal son was an allegory to our Father in heaven. Just as God adds lost souls to His church on the basis of obedience to the gospel, God also welcomes the wayward child back into the family on the basis of repentance.

A restoration among brothers and sisters in the home congregation must also take place. When a brother who has been overtaken by sin decides to come back to the church, Christians are not to act like the older brother acted toward the prodigal son. "For if a man think himself to be something, when he is nothing, he deceiveth himself" (Galatians 6:3).

Instead of putting ourselves above our erring brother, we are to put ourselves "in his shoes" and restore him in a spirit of meekness. Upon his repentance, we are to view his relationship with the church the way it formerly was and ought to have been all along.

However, this restored relationship with the church cannot take place without the erring brother first having his relationship with God restored. Christians have fellowship with one another through the fellowship they each have with God (see 1 John 1:3; 1 Corinthians 1:9). If fellowship with God has been broken, it has also been broken with the church.

The church cannot extend fellowship to a person who is not in fellowship with God. To do so would be to usurp God's authority under the pretense that we are more merciful than Him! When this happens, the wayward is only "restored" under a false premise and is given a false sense of security. A life cannot be right until it is made right with God.

Why Is Restoration Needed?

An erring child must be restored to God because of their sad condition. Our wayward brethren have no fellowship with God. "If we say that we have fellowship with him, and walk in darkness, we lie, and do not the truth" (1 John 1:6).

The erring brother who goes on continuing in sin has no remaining sacrifice for sin:

"For if we sin wilfully after that we have received the knowledge of the truth, there remaineth no more sacrifice for sins, But a certain fearful looking for of judgment and fiery indignation, which shall devour the adversaries" (Hebrews 10:26).

A wayward brother is a lost soul (Matthew 16:26). He has a shipwrecked faith (1 Timothy 1:19-20). He is undoubtedly in a worse condition than before: "For if after they have escaped the pollutions of the world through the knowledge of the Lord and Saviour Jesus Christ, they are again entangled therein, and overcome, the latter end is worse with them than the beginning. For it had been better for them not to have known the way of righteousness, than, after they have known it, to turn from the holy commandment delivered unto them. But it is happened unto them according to the true proverb, the dog is turned to his own vomit again; and the sow that was washed to her wallowing in the mire" (2 Peter 2:20-22).

When Should Restoration Occur?

The wayward person comes home through the same door he left. If he left because he was never grounded in the faith, then study must take place, and he must become grounded. If he was never truly converted, then he must be truly converted.

➤ If the wayward would rather be doing something recreational on Sundays, then he must be convinced of the error and sinfulness of this judgment and repent.

➤ If work has taken the wayward away from the church, the he must find another job. It is better to enter in heaven unemployed, than to enter into hell making a million dollars a year!

➤ If a spouse has taken the wayward away from the church, then let us convert the spouse as well as the wayward. The wayward must come to value no relationship above the relationship he has with Christ.

➤ If the wayward has been upset at something or someone in the church, then they must go to that person and settle the matter with Christian maturity (Matthew 18:15 ff.).

➤ If the wayward has coveted some sin or sinful activity more than a relationship with the Lord, he must repent of this sin and be made right with God before he can be made right with the church.

➤ If the wayward moved to a new area and never identified with a congregation in that place, let him repent of this idleness, identify with a sound congregation, and go to work!

> If the wayward has "just quit going" then let us exhort him to be faithful and impress upon him the severity of his lost condition.

Remember, the church cannot extend restoration on a congregational basis until God has restored fellowship with the wayward on the basis of repentance. A congregation cannot enjoy fellowship with a wayward brother who is not in fellowship with God (see 2 Thessalonians 3:6).

We are thus commanded, not to hurt or because we hate our erring brethren, but to save them (cf. 1 Corinthians 5:5). We love our wayward brethren and consider them our brethren, but we also plead with them to come home before it is eternally too late.

By inspiration, James considered the erring brother a sinner and instructed Christians of the need to convert such a one:

"Brethren, if any of you do err from the truth, and one convert him; Let him know, that he which converteth the sinner from the error of his way shall save a soul from death, and shall hide a multitude of sins" (James 5:19-20).

We must convince our brother of his need to repent rather than console him in his sins. Paul did not console the erring brother at Corinth while he was living in his sin of fornication (see 1 Corinthians 5:1-13). Rather, Paul rebuked this brother as well as the church at Corinth for being puffed up in this brother's sin (1 Corinthians 5:2).

They were commanded to purge themselves of this brother and his sinful ways (1 Corinthians 5:7 ff.). The church could not fellowship this man who had forsaken his fellowship with God. The erring brother was to be removed, hoping this would lead to his spirit being saved in the day of Christ (1 Corinthians 5:5).

Paul did not hate this brother or the congregation. In fact, this was a difficult, bitter, and sorrowful thing for him to address. He wanted this man and the church to know the severity of this sin and that his soul was in jeopardy. Paul's intent is made clear by studying in 2 Corinthians 2:1-8, as is his instruction for the congregational restoration of this man: "But I determined this with myself, that I would not come again to you in heaviness. For if I make you sorry, who is he then that maketh me glad, but the same which is made sorry by me? And I wrote this same unto you, lest, when I came, I should have sorrow from them of whom I ought to rejoice; having confidence in you all, that my joy is the joy of you all. For out of much affliction and anguish of heart I wrote unto you with many tears; not that ye should be grieved, **but that ye might know the love which I have more abundantly unto you**. But if any have caused grief, he hath not grieved me, but in part: that I may not overcharge you all. Sufficient to such a man is this punishment, which was inflicted of many. So that contrariwise ye ought rather to forgive him, and comfort him, lest perhaps such a one should be swallowed up with overmuch sorrow. Wherefore I beseech you that ye would confirm your love toward him."

It was because Paul loved this congregation and the soul of this erring brother that he instructed them to put him away from the church. The reason: (1) so that the erring brother might be saved (1 Corinthians 5:5); (2) to test their obedience in all things (2 Corinthians 2:9); and (3) so that the congregation might be cleared of any wrongdoing in the matter (2 Corinthians 7:11); (4) so that the evil influence of sin would not spread as leaven throughout the church (1 Corinthians 5:6 ff.).

How Can Christians Better Restore Erring Brethren?

The Lord has commanded us to resolve conflicts with our erring brethren (see Matthew 18:15-17). Do you think we could restore more brethren if we talked to our brethren, as Christ commanded, instead of talking about our brethren? Great harm is caused by gossip and a congregation with a gossiping spirit will never flourish!

We must save these souls if at all possible. As concerned members of God's family, we should warn and pray for the erring (Matthew 18:15-17). We cannot admonish the wayward Christian as a brother (1 Thessalonians 5:14), if we never talk to him.

Wayward brethren are the responsibility of all who are spiritual (Galatians 6:1). However, a new preacher in a congregation should especially take an interest in those who have left the Lord. Usually, those who are considering leaving the church will drift away between preacher changes.

Elders should meet with their new preacher to discuss the brethren who have gone back into the world. They must not be allowed to leave that easily. The erring must be restored if at all possible. Saving the erring should be a primary concern to any congregation.

Sometimes a new preacher can help to restore wayward members simply because there is no embarrassing history between them. A prospect list should be formed and visits should be conducted as soon as possible.

Elders, however, are the shepherds of the flock. They must have a heart to seek the lost sheep and return them to the fold. Any man who does not possess such a heart cannot be qualified to serve as an elder. Too many times elders become pre-occupied with everything but restoring the wayward. Safeguarding the sheep must be priority #1.

In Conclusion

Let us always remember we are to be holy, for the Lord is holy (Leviticus 11:44; 1 Peter 1:16). God has a holy will for the conduct of His church (1 Timothy 3:15).

The erring Christian is still a child a God, nevertheless, in rebellious error. Our devotion to this brother should reflect our devotion to God. Let us remember how Christ died for that lost brother who is in need of restoration (Romans 14:15). The love we display to him should be a clear manifestation of the fruit of the Spirit in our lives and our loyalty to the redeeming work of our Savior.

When wayward Christians are restored let us rejoice! Let us comfort them with a spirit of meekness and love them as our brothers, realizing the unspeakable grace of God almighty, while appreciating the courage of our fallen brother who has come admitting his wrongs and seeking to be renewed in his fellowship with God and the church.

May we always be kind and tenderhearted (Ephesians 4:31-32), considering even ourselves (Galatians 6:1-2), as we seek to restore the erring according to the word of the Lord.

"Restore unto me the joy of thy salvation; and uphold me with thy free spirit" (Psalm 51:12).

Discussion Questions for Chapter Twenty-Four

1.) Use this time to discuss some brethren who are in error and need to be restored in your home congregation or community.

2.) What has taken them away from the church?

3.) Including the elders, and even the preacher, who else can go to speak with the wayward?

4.) When do you plan to go?

25
Congregational Responsibilities

God commands and expects a congregation of His people to perform out of that which they have (2 Corinthians 8:11-12). In His righteousness, God also assures us He will only expect of us and judge us according to what we have.

However, God's expectations do not offer congregations a crutch or an excuse to be slack in doing what He has commanded. Be assured that God requires and expects faithfulness from every congregation of His people – especially with regard to teaching and preaching His word.

Instead of making excuses, every congregation of the Lord's church needs to be considering the responsibility they have as Christians, both unto Christ and unto their fellow man and work with a readiness to will and perform out of that which they have (2 Corinthians 8:11).

Every Member Has a Responsibility

Every Christian should be found asking, "What is my responsibility?" We should especially ask this question in the context of church growth.

What is my responsibility as it pertains to the growth – both spiritual and numerical – of my home congregation? It is this author's conviction that a congregation will never grow and reach its full potential without likeminded and faithful brethren *first asking* this essential question.

Just as God's promise to Joshua came with conditions, certain obstacles, and responsibilities for his and future generations (Joshua 1:7-9), God's promise to us comes with conditions, certain obstacles, and responsibilities both for this and future generations.

"Go ye" is not a command *only* for preachers. Every joint and every member has something to supply and a work to accomplish unto the building up of the body of Christ (Ephesians 4:16). Church growth and personal evangelism requires teamwork and support from within the church.

Carefully note some of the various "one another" passages as they often apply to evangelism:

> Consider *one another* to provoke unto love and good works (Hebrews 10:24).

> Be of the same mind *one toward another* (Romans 12:16).

> Edify *one another* (Romans 14:19). This same truth is revealed in Ephesians 4:16.

> Admonish *one another* (Romans 15:14; Colossians 3:16).

> Serve *one another* (Galatians 5:13).

> Bear the burdens of *one another* (Galatians 6:2).

> Forbear and forgive *one another* (Ephesians 4:2; Colossians 3:13).

➢ Be kind *one to another* (Ephesians 4:32).

➢ Submit *one to another* (Ephesians 5:21; 1 Peter 5:5).

➢ Lie not *one to another* (Colossians 3:9), but speak truth *one to another* (Ephesians 4:25), not evil (James 4:11).

➢ Comfort *one another* (1 Thessalonians 4:18).

➢ Have compassion for *one another* (1 Peter 3:8-9).

➢ Grudge not *one against another* (James 5:9).

➢ Confess faults *one to another* (James 5:16).

The phrase "one another" is an inclusive phrase which signifies to us that the responsibility is to be shared by every member. Each of these admonitions requires love and a Christ-like spirit to obey. A congregation which has these qualities will grow because of them. When Christians act according to these "one another" passages, they attract others and bring out the best in others.

The Deterrent of Worldliness

Every member has a responsibility to live above the world and the lusts therein (1 John 2:15-17). The church today must rise above our love for the here-and-now. Just as a Christ-like spirit will attract others and bring out the best in them, the spirit of the world will turn others from the church and bring out the worst in them.

Unfortunately, some Christians have just enough religion to make them miserable. They know what they need to do, but are made miserable by their desire to keep living in the lusts of the world (Romans 6:12; 8:13; 12:1). We cannot serve God while living in the devil's kingdom.

How are we any different from the world when we:

➢ Turn a blind eye to sin;

➢ Live in adultery;

➢ Consume alcohol recreationally or socially;

➢ Dress in immodest apparel;

➢ Are absent at church assemblies;

➢ Never take part in the work of the church;

➢ Fail to contribute generously and sacrificially of our means;

➢ Gossip and backbite faithful Christians;

➢ Covet the treasures of the world more than the treasures of heaven;

➢ Never speak a word about Christ to the lost souls we encounter everyday?

Which of these things would you be comfortable doing when the Lord comes again? Nothing will kill the prospects of church growth quicker and ruin a congregation's name in the community faster than a bunch of immoral hypocrites playing church of Sunday morning.

Who would want to be a part of a group like that? As a congregation of God's people we have a responsibility to live godly in this present age (Titus 2:11-12). We must make a clean break with the devil. We cannot compromise with evil and expect that good will come.

To Fail to Plan is to Plan to Fail

Every member should strive to work together in forming a plan for growth and following through. We should have a primary method and a backup plan. Some people may not be comfortable with a one-on-one Bible study, but would be interested in studying from VHS or DVD lessons.

Whatever the method, the aim is to teach them the truth. If your congregation needs help learning how to use these resources, plan for someone to come a provide training.

Form and work from a prospect list (Mark 6:19). And don't forget to be patient, endure, and persevere (Luke 8:15; 1 Corinthians 15:58).

Rather than compete with each other, work together in bringing souls to Christ. Congregations will accomplish more and greater good if each member will work together and pull in the same direction. Competition among ideas and agendas can often lead to good works being sabotaged by immature and divisive Christians.

Every Preacher Has a Responsibility

The preacher's responsibilities are summed up in Paul's commands to Timothy, "Preach the word...do the work of an evangelist" (2 Timothy 4:2, 5). If you are not willing to preach the word, *do not preach*! Peter commanded, "If any man speak, let him speak as the oracles of God" (1 Peter 4:11).

Lost souls will only find the redemption they seek when men of integrity teach them the oracles of God. Disobedient preachers who confine their lessons to opinions and bragging should consider that souls are not saved on the basis of "I think so" and "Listen to what I did." Souls are saved upon obeying as, "Thus said the Lord." Do the work of an evangelist and preach the word.

Peter also wrote, "If any man minister, let him do it as of the ability which God giveth" (1 Peter 4:11b). Preachers must labor for the Lord according to the ability they have rather than attempting to be a carbon copy of a preacher down the road. The congregation must support and encourage their preacher to use his God-given ability.

A preacher should find consolation in serving a congregation that wants him as their preacher. If a preacher happens not to be a suitable fit for that congregation, perhaps he should look elsewhere and give those brethren the opportunity to find a satisfactory man. Every preacher should serve where he feels like he is free to serve faithfully with the ability God has given him.

Glorify God. Preachers must preach the word and labor with the ability God has given so that, "God in all things may be glorified through Jesus Christ, to whom be praise and dominion for ever and ever. Amen" (1 Peter 4:11c). Perhaps the greatest need in the church today is for each member to refocus our attention upon the glorifying of God. Congregations who do not seek God's glory and seek not to glorify God are destined for failure – including every soul therein which would promote and support such a sinful scheme.

Concerning church growth, preachers need to provide a spark for their respective congregations. The preacher shouldn't be expected to be the engine driving the machine, but he should be the spark plug. Let him be an encourager – both publically and privately.

Every Deacon Should Have a Responsibility

A deacon must be proven to be qualified for the work of a deacon according to God's qualifications (1Timothy 3:8-13). He must also be proven to be a deacon by his service in the church.

A man must not be a deacon in title only or simply for the sake of claiming, "We have deacons." Every deacon should be appointed because the eldership has a certain need for him and a specific work in mind.

It is troubling to see a congregation "subcontract" many good works while deacons are barely being used, if at all. Why have deacons if they have no service(s) to which they can devote themselves? Let us study carefully the sixth chapter of Acts and its first seven verses:

"And in those days, when the number of the disciples was multiplied, there arose a murmuring of the Grecians against the Hebrews, because their widows were neglected in the daily ministration. Then the twelve called the multitude of the disciples unto them, and said, It is not reason that we should leave the word of God, and serve tables. Wherefore, brethren, look ye out among you seven men of honest report, full of the Holy Ghost and wisdom, whom we may appoint over this business. But we will give ourselves continually to prayer, and to the ministry of the word. And the saying pleased the whole multitude: and they chose Stephen, a man full of faith and of the Holy Ghost, and Philip, and Prochorus, and Nicanor, and Timon, and Parmenas, and Nicolas a proselyte of Antioch: Whom they set before the apostles: and when they had prayed, they laid their hands on them. And the word of God increased; and the number of the disciples multiplied in Jerusalem greatly; and a great company of the priests were obedient to the faith."

Although this passage never mentions the word "deacon," we can agree on the importance of the apostles' decision. By delegating this important work to godly men, the apostles were able to devote themselves to the preaching of the gospel.

The result of such teamwork was an increase in the number of disciples, even including a great number of the priests. Converting these priests probably took a considerable amount of time and study which could not have been given had this work of waiting tables not been delegated.

Herein, we learn of a specific work which the apostles had in mind, which required a certain character and quality of man, which enabled the apostles to continue devoting themselves to the ministry of the word. From this passage, the Bible student can understand the precedent being set which clearly illustrates a parallel to what these men did and the importance of the deacon's work today. Such a man, if he is used correctly and puts his talents to work, can fulfill his responsibilities and play an important role in the growth of a congregation.

Every Elder Has a Responsibility

Elders are God's ordained shepherds or pastors in each local congregation (1 Peter 5:1-4; Acts 14:23). The terms "shepherd," "elder," and "pastor" refer to the same office (Ephesians 4:11).

These terms are not given by God to serve as religious titles, as denominations have done, but as job descriptions for the office. The same could be said of every office in the church (e.g. "apostles" were ones sent with the message, "prophets" prophesied, "ministers" or "evangelists" preach the gospel and "deacons" serve).

Elders "feed the flock" (Acts 20:28; 1 Peter 5:2a), hence they are called "pastors" (Ephesians 4:11). Elders "oversee" the flock (Acts 20:28; Hebrews 13:7, 17; 1 Peter 5:2b), hence they are called "overseers."

If one in the flock goes astray, the shepherds have the primary responsibility of seeking and admonishing the straying sheep. If one comes wanting to place membership from another congregation, the overseers have the primary responsibility of making sure it is not a wolf in sheep's clothing or that the person is not secretly bringing sin "into the camp."

Multiplied elderships are failing in these aspects of their God-ordained responsibilities. Knowing this to be true, we ought always to show a great love, admiration, appreciation, and affection toward those righteous men who faithfully accept and honor God's instructions for this tremendous responsibility.

As we have discussed in a previous chapter, in too many places the preacher has become the "pastor." We practice what we preach against. If elders will shepherd the flock, the preacher can do the work of an evangelist much more effectively by spending his time working to convert new souls to Christ.

James A. Harding had a very biblical view of the work of elders and preachers – one that is not being implemented very much today. Brother Harding was not against full-time preachers, as some have supposed. Brother Harding was against the pastoral system we have been using in the Lord's church.

Rather than making a shepherd out of the preacher, he believed it was the elder's work to teach and preach on Sundays, as well as visit among the congregation. If the elders wanted to hire a full-time preacher, they should let him go into the area and work to convert souls with evangelistic efforts. In this case, the preacher would be conducting cottage meetings, brush arbor meetings, tent meetings, etc., while the elders took care of the work in the local congregation.

I do not believe we will ever see Harding's plan implemented on a wide-scale basis in this country among existing congregations, but perhaps we will see it implemented more in the mission field. However we continue, elders must recognize they are ordained to oversee souls first – the budget and the building are of secondary importance.

In Conclusion

Are we members of a congregation which faithfully accepts its responsibilities? Are we Christians who faithfully accept our responsibilities? If we answered "NO" to either question, we must obey Christ and "Remember therefore from whence thou art fallen, and repent, and do the first works" (Revelation 2:5).

Life is too short to spend it in willful neglect of the life God would have us to live. Such a manner of life is sinning against God. "Therefore to him that knoweth to do good, and doeth it not, to him it is sin" (James 4:17).

Read carefully what Christ will say to those on His left hand. Many souls will be lost forever because of their willful neglect to do what they knew to be right: "Then shall he say also unto them on the left hand, Depart from me, ye cursed, into everlasting fire, prepared for the devil and his angels: For I was an hungred, and ye gave me no meat: I was thirsty, and ye gave me no drink: I was a stranger, and ye took me not in: naked, and ye clothed me not: sick, and in prison, and ye visited me not. Then shall they also answer him, saying, Lord, when saw we thee an hungred, or athirst, or a stranger, or naked, or sick, or in prison, and did not minister unto thee? Then shall he answer them, saying, Verily I say unto you, Inasmuch as ye did it not to one of the least of these, ye did it not to me. And these shall go away into everlasting punishment: but the righteous into life eternal" (Matthew 25:41-46).

To neglect our responsibilities in Christ is to live willfully in sin. "If we sin willfully after that we have received the

287

knowledge of the truth, there remains no more sacrifice for sins, but a certain fearful looking for of judgment and fiery indignation, which shall devour the adversaries" (Hebrews 10:26-27).

Are we producing fruit? Or, are we dead on the vine? Shall we willfully neglect to obey the responsibilities given by God? Or, shall we cry out, "Here am I, send me!" Whatever our role is in our home congregation, let us be faithful and serve the Lord!

"Speak, Lord; for thy servant heareth." (1 Samuel 3:9).

Discussion Questions for Chapter Twenty-Five

1.) Discuss the importance of asking, "What is my responsibility?"

2.) Discuss the responsibility of the preacher; of the deacon; of the elder.

3.) Discuss how the church will grow when every member is working together to fulfill their responsibilities.

4.) Discuss the differences between being the church and playing church.

26
What Do You Want to Do?

A person will be faithful in doing only what he or she sincerely wants to do. *We do what we want to do?* If we have truly obeyed the gospel, it is because obeying the Lord truly was what we wanted to do. If we truly are walking in Christ's light this very hour, it is because Christ's light is our truest desire. To be sincerely faithful to God, we must make God's commandments our sincerest desires.

Man Cannot be Forced or Manipulated into Obeying God

We have studied that man cannot be manipulated, forced, or deceived into obeying the gospel. One will not find manipulation, force, or deception in God's plan for saving souls. We help the lost by allowing them the opportunity to judge their lives personally from the word of God. We hope to open the Scriptures and reveal God's will to them through study of the sacred word. We also hope to reveal God to them as His light reflects off of us.

Man Cannot be Forced or Manipulated into Evangelism

Just as it is impossible for a Christian to manipulate or force obedience upon another, no one can manipulate or force a Christian into the necessary obedience of the Great Commission.

We must obey the Lord because that is our sincerest desire. No one can force a Christian to win souls. We either *will* or we *will not*; and only we can decide what we will do.

God Only Accepts Sincere Acts of Obedience

Throughout the Scriptures we find that God only accepts sincere acts of obedience. It was true with Cain; it is true with us.

Whatever man does in service to God must be done from the heart and from the Bible. The gospel must be obeyed from the heart (Romans 6:17). If one is manipulated, forced, or deceived it is not obedience from the heart. The disposition of the heart must be right for the act to be pleasing to God.

God must be worshipped from the heart and from the Bible – in spirit and truth (John 4:24). Such is true worship according to the Lord. He only accepts true worship. For the worship to be true, so too must be the heart and the actions of the worshipper.

Christ must be loved from the heart – in sincerity (Ephesians 6:24) – and from the Bible. To love the Lord is to obey Him (John 14:15). It is neither love nor obedience if it is not sincere.

Man must obey God with the right attitude *and* action. It takes both. To have the right action with the wrong attitude is to be superficial and hypocritical. To have the right attitude and commit the wrong action is to be sincerely wrong. To love and obey is to have the right attitude and the right action.

As soul winners we must have the right attitude and action. Our attitude must be one of devotion and faithfulness to Christ. Our actions must be derived from the word of God.

Man Will Sincerely Obey Only What He Chooses to Obey

Everyone is serving someone, whether it is self and sin or whether it is God and righteousness (Romans 6:16). Ask yourself, "Who am I choosing to obey?"

Do we sincerely want to obey God? Do we truly love Him? If so, why delay in sharing our love for Him and the love we enjoy through Him?

Who do we obey when we refuse or neglect to keep Christ's mission alive? Can one be a faithful child of God while refusing to share the teachings of His Son? Will the faithful or unfaithful receive a crown of life when life is over (Revelation 2:10)?

When we speak of "the world" being lost and dying in sin, we speak of our friends, our neighbors, our parents, our brothers, our sisters, and possibly our children. To reach these precious loved ones, the Lord has ordered His church, "Go and preach." God has assured us we will save some (1 Corinthians 9:22) and Christ has assured us He will be with us (Matthew 28:20; Mark 16:20).

Every child of God has a decision to make. What will be our decision? Will we stand and be numbered? Will we claim victory through sharing the gospel of hope? Will we obey the Lord by loving Him sincerely and obediently? What do we want to do? What do we want to be?

293

Do we want to be soul winners? Do we want to be found sowing and watering the seed of the kingdom? What do you want to do with your faith?

One cannot run and hide from such questions. Although we may resist obeying Christ and fulfilling our duties and responsibilities as Christians, one day we will each appear before His judgment seat (2 Corinthians 5:10). Each of us is accountable to God (Romans 14:12).

Now is the time to consider the answer we must give. Now is the time to repent if necessary. Now is the time to encourage brethren in every place to put on the whole armor of God and gain the victory! Now is the time to stop *playing* church and to *be* the church!

In Conclusion

We could have just as easily placed this chapter first as last in our study. The things we have stated in this chapter are fundamental to our becoming soul winners. If we do not want to be soul winners, we will never be soul winners. The desire has to be there.

The fields remain white and ready to harvest. The Lord is in need of laborers. Will we not choose to be laborers in the noblest work mortal man has ever known? Will our faith shine forth as the sun in a world ever darkening by the shadows of immorality and sin?

As we go throughout this world, will we take the gospel? Will we go armed to battle Satan and equipped to help the lost?

Someone very faithful to God once loved us and helped us to obey the truth. Now, when we are needed most, let us stop at nothing to see that the lost loved ones we know have the same opportunity to hear the gospel. May we never stop at words! What do you want to do?

Produce no fruit for the Savior and be "hewn down and cast into the fire" (Matthew 3:10; 7:19). Each one of us will someday stand before Christ and give an account for the life we chose to live (Romans 2:6; Revelation 20:11-13).

On that day, would we rather hear, "Come, ye blessed of my Father, inherit the kingdom prepared for you from the foundation of the world," *or* "Depart from me, ye cursed, into everlasting fire, prepared for the devil and his angels" (Matthew 25:34, 41). Heaven or hell – which shall we choose? What do you want to do?

On that appointed day, how sad it would be to stand before the King, arm in arm with loved ones, while on His left hand. Our loved ones would be standing there because they never obeyed the gospel and we would be standing condemned because we never cared enough to teach them.

We must repent of our apathy before it is eternally too late. Let us work "while it is day, for the night cometh when no man can work" (John 9:4).

God, in His grace, has given us today – not guaranteeing tomorrow – but giving today. What will we do with today? The Lord needs us *today*! Lost souls need us *today*!

As we go, we may be oft disappointed. From time to time, we may ask ourselves, "Why bother?" We may come near to losing hope in our fellow man and possibly even our brethren.

If heartbreak was all we could say about soul winning, surely it would be a foolish and futile thought to entertain. Thankfully, it is not! We also know the joy and excitement that is shared with those souls who decide to pledge themselves to Christ as they obey His blessed gospel. To know that we have had even some small role in a precious name being added to the Lamb's Book of Life makes every trial and ridicule worthwhile. Now, what do you want to do?

Realizing our value in God's eternal purpose, let us unite with joy in our salvation, share in the cause of winning souls, and praise God for His glorious favor.

As the links to this world are broken one by one and our passage is soothed into another world, we cannot help but to realize that soon we too must rest from our labors. Our works shall follow and His face we shall see. Let us glory in His coming, find faith in His might, and ever look with an eager expectation toward the heavens, knowing that some day, yes some day, our Lord shall return "with clouds; and every eye shall see Him, and they also which pierced Him: and all kindreds of the earth shall wail because of Him. Even so, Amen" (Revelation 1:7).

May God bless you, my brethren, as you walk in His light and trust in His grace! May the day of the Lord find you singing redemption's sweet song!

Finally, my brethren, if we never meet this side of glory, may we meet someday soon in that blessed land which knows no parting, where God is its Light and our faith has become sight.

"The grace of our Lord Jesus Christ be with you all. Amen" (Revelation 22:21).

Discussion Questions for Chapter Twenty-Six

1.) In what manner must we obey God?

2.) Who are we obeying when we neglect or refuse to keep Christ's mission alive?

3.) What will be the final judgment upon all who have disobeyed Christ?

4.) What do you want to do with your life?

Part Three: Each One Reach One
Bible Study Lessons

Lesson One: Who Is the Lord?

"Who is the Lord, that I should obey his voice...?"
-Pharaoh (Exodus 5:2)

1.) Psalm 53:1: It is foolish not to believe in God **True or False**

2.) Hebrews 11:6: In order to be pleasing to God, we must believe that He exists and that He rewards those who diligently seek Him. **True or False**

3.) Acts 14:15-17: God's existence can be proven by His creation. **True or False**

4.) Genesis 1:1; Psalm 19:1: God is the Creator of the heavens, the earth, and all things therein. His creation declares His glory. **True or False**

5.) Matthew 6:24-34: God has created life, but He is not active today. **True or False**

6.) John 3:16; 1 John 4:16: God is love and so loved the world that He sent His only Son. **True or False**

7.) Isaiah 59:1, 2; 2 Corinthians 5:17-21: Man has no need to be reconciled to God. **True or False**

8.) 2 Peter 3:9; Acts 17:30: It is God's will that man repent (turn) from his sins and serve Him. **True or False**

9.) 1 Peter 1:16; 1 Peter 2:21: God is holy and commands you and me to be holy by following the example of Christ. **True or False**

10.) Acts 22:14; 1 John 1:9; Revelation 15:3; Hebrews 2:2: God's judgements are always right **True or False**

11.) Acts 17:31; Psalm 19:9; Hebrews 10:30-31: God is righteous and will judge this world by His righteousness. **True or False**

12.) 1 Peter 3:12: The eyes of the Lord are over the righteous and His ears are open to their cries, but His face is set against those who live in unrighteousness. **True or False**

Review:
Give at least three attributes of God studied in this lesson and discuss how these attributes affect your salvation.

Lesson Two: What Is Man?

"What is man, that thou art mindful of him?"
-A Psalm of David (Psalm 8:4)

1.) **Psalm 139:14; Genesis 2:7:** Man is a fearfully and wonderfully created being. **True or False**

2.) **Genesis 1:26; 2 Corinthians 5:1; 2 Peter 1:14; Ecclesiastes 12:7:** Man is a spiritual being temporarily housed in a mortal body. **True or False**

3.) **Hebrews 9:27; John 5:28-29; 2 Corinthians 5:10:** Every man will cease to exist at death. **True or False**

4.) **Matthew 16:26:** A person's soul is their most valuable possession. **True or False**

5.) **Luke 12:13-21; James 4:14; 1 Peter 1:24-25:** Life is brief and tomorrow is not guaranteed. **True or False**

6.) **Ecclesiastes 12:13-14:** The meaning of life is to have a good time! **True or False**

7.) **Mark 12:29-31:** Man's love for God and his neighbor are not really that important. **True or False**

8.) **John 1:9:** Man is not born in the light of Christ; but a he is born a sinner. **True or False**

9.) **Ezekiel 18:20:** Man must be first able to sin in order to be a sinner. **True or False**

10.) Romans 7:9: A man is alive in his relationship with God as a child and before he sins. **True or False**

11.) Luke 15:24; Ephesians 2:1; Romans 6:23; Isaiah 59:1-2: A person's own sin causes a spiritual death or separation between him and God. **True or False**

12.) John 3:3-5: Because of this spiritual death or separation through sin, sinful people must be born again and reconciled to God. **True or False**

Review:
Give at least three attributes of man and discuss how these affect your salvation.

Lesson Three: What Is Truth?

"What is truth?"

-Pilate (John 18:38)

1.) 2 Corinthians 5:19: The gospel of Christ is the word of reconciliation. **True or False**

2.) Psalm119:151; John 17:17: God's word is always true. **True or False**

3.) Romans 1:16-17: God's righteousness and power to save man is taught in the gospel. **True or False**

4.) Mark 7:1-13: Manmade traditions are safe to follow as a religious guide and are equivalent to the word of God. **True or False**

5.) 2 Timothy 3:16-17; John 16:13: All scripture is given by God for doctrine and every good work. **True or False**

Traditions of Men (Mark 7:1-13)	Word of God (2 Timothy 3:16-17)
Hypocrisy	Doctrine
Hearts Far from God	Reproof
Vain Worship	Correction
Lay Aside the Command-ment of God	Instruction in Righteousness
Reject the Commandment of God	Make You Perfect
Make the Word of God Void – of no effect	Thoroughly Furnish (Equip) unto Every Good Work

6.) **Proverbs 14:12; Jeremiah 10:23:** Opinions, emotions, and feelings are a safe guide for knowing the truth. **True or False**

7.) **Matthew 7:13-14; Matthew 27:15-26:** Man will be saved by following the actions of the majority. **True or False**

8.) **Colossians 2:8:** Manmade philosophies are a safe guide for religion. **True or False**

9.) **John 12:48; John 8:32; James 1:21:** Man must receive the word of the Lord in order to be made free from his sins. **True or False**

10.) **1 Peter 1:22-25:** If a person will obey God's word his soul will be purified from sins. **True or False**

Review:
Explain the differences between manmade religious traditions and the word of God. What are some examples of such traditions today? Can these traditions save you?

Lesson Four: What Must I Do to be Saved?

"Sirs, what must I do to be saved?"
-The Philippian Jailor (Acts 16:30)

1.) **Matthew 7:21-27; Luke 6:46:** Man is saved by being a good person. Obedience to God is not necessary **True or False**

2.) **John 10:27; John 14:15; 1 John 2:3-4**: One can love Christ without obeying Him. **True or False**

1.) **Romans 10:17; John 5:39; 2 Timothy 2:15:** Man must hear and study the word of God. **True or False**

2.) **Hebrews 11:6; John 8:24; 2 Thessalonians 2:12:** It doesn't matter if you believe in God. **True or False**

3.) **Luke 13:3-5; Acts 3:19; 2 Peter 3:9:** Everyone sins. God knows this and doesn't expect us to change. **True or False**

4.) **Matthew 10:32-33; Romans 10:9-10:** Man must confess his faith in Christ to be saved. **True or False**

5.) **Galatians 3:26-27; Romans 6:3-7; Colossians 2:12-13:** Man must be baptized into Christ. **True or False**

6.) **Ephesians 1:3, 7; 2 Timothy 2:10:** Man must be in Christ to receive all spiritual blessings including redemption and salvation. **True or False**

7.) **Acts 2:38-41, 47; Acts 22:16; Mark 16:15-16:** A person doesn't have to be baptized in order to be saved. **True or False**

8.) **Hebrews 8:12; Hebrews 10:17:** When one is saved, his sins are remembered no more. **True or False**

9.) **Ephesians 2:12:** We have no hope for forgiveness outside of Christ. **True or False**

10.) **Matthew 28:18-20:** Each of the passages we have studied emphasizes different commandments. Man must not pick and choose which ones he will obey, but rather he must obey *all* Christ has commanded. **True or False**

Review:
State and explain what the Bible teaches man must do to be saved and become a Christian. How is the teaching of the Bible different from what you have been taught or believed? What do you believe to be true now?

Lesson Five: What Manner of Persons Ought You to Be?

"...what manner of persons ought ye to be in all holy conversation and godliness...?"

-Peter (2 Peter 3:11-12)

1.) **2 Peter 3:10-12:** Holiness and godliness can be overlooked, as long as you are well-liked by others. **True or False**

2.) **Romans 6:1-2; Hebrews 10:26-31:** Sin is not a big deal to Christians. We are once saved and always saved and can never fall from grace. **True or False**

3.) **Hebrews 5:12-14:** It is God's will that we mature spiritually to the point of becoming teachers and becoming more able to discern good from evil. **True or False**

4.) **2 Peter 1:5-11:** It is God's will that we continue adding to our faith by maturing and growing in the virtues of the Christian faith. **True or False**

5.) **Jude 3; 2 John 9-11; 1 Peter 3:15:** It is not important to stand against false doctrine, because that can make enemies for us. **True or False**

6.) **Hebrews 4:14-16; James 1:12; James 4:7-8; 1 Peter 5:5-7:** When faced with temptation, Christians must endure by approaching the throne of grace, casting all our cares and burdens on God, and depending on Him to deliver us. **True or False**

309

7.) 1 John 1:5-2:2: It is God's will that we continue to walk in the light of His word, have fellowship with the church, confess our sins to Him and ask His forgiveness. **True or False**

8.) John 4:24-26: It doesn't matter how you worship, just as long as you like it. **True or False**

Worship in Spirit and Truth

Act	Spirit (attitude)	Truth (action)
Lord's Supper **1 Cor. 11:17-34**	Examine self	Unleavened bread, fruit of vine, first day of week
Prayer **Luke 11:1-4; John 14:13**	Thanksgiving; humility	To God through Christ
Singing **Eph. 5:19-20; Col. 3:16-17**	Grace in the heart	Singing, spiritual songs, everyone
Giving **1 Cor. 16:1-2 2 Cor. 9:6-11**	Cheerfully with purpose	A collection, as prospered, first day of week
Preaching **2 Co. 4:5; Ep. 4:15; Jas. 1:21; 1 Pt. 4:11**	In love with meekness; receive with meekness	Speak truth, preach Christ not self

9.) Hebrews 10:24; Hebrews 13:1; 1 Peter 1:22: It is God's will that Christians continue to love and encourage one another. **True or False**

10.) Galatians 5:16-26: Christians are to walk after the Spirit of God, and not to fulfill the lusts of the flesh. **True or False**

11.) **1 Corinthians 15:58; Galatians 6:7-10:** It is God's will that we keep the mission of Christ alive by being steadfast and untiring in the work of the Lord. **True or False**

12.) **Matthew 5:13-16:** Once you have obeyed the gospel you are to be an influence for good and righteousness in this world. **True or False**

Review:

Explain and discuss the responsibilities of being a Christian. Is the Christian religion a wholehearted religion?

51254498R00179

Made in the USA
San Bernardino, CA
17 July 2017